DATE DUE

FOLLETT

Engel v. Vitale

Prayer in the Public Schools

by Julia C. Loren

FAMOUS

TRIALS

Lucent Books, San Diego, CA

Titles in the Famous Trials series include:

The Boston Massacre

Brown v. Board of Education

Cherokee Nation v. Georgia

The Dred Scott Decision

The Impeachment of Bill
  Clinton

Miranda v. Arizona

The Nuremberg Trials

The O.J. Simpson Trial

Roe v. Wade

The Salem Witch Trials

The Scopes Trial

The Trial of Adolf Eichmann

The Trial of Joan of Arc

The Trial of John Brown

The Trial of Socrates

*The editors wish to thank Don Nardo for his
valuable contribution to this book.*

Library of Congress Cataloging-in-Publication Data

Loren, Julia C.
    Engel v. Vitale : prayer in the public schools /
by Julia C. Loren
    p. cm. — (Famous trials)
    Includes bibliographical references and index.
    Summary: Points out that although a 1962 Supreme Court
case decided that official prayers in public schools are
unconstitutional, the issue of separation of church and
state remains.
    ISBN 1-56006-732-2 (alk. paper)
    1. Engel, Steven I.—Trials, litigation, etc.—Juvenile
literature. 2. Vitale, William J.—Trials, litigation, etc.—
Juvenile literature. 3. Prayer in the public schools—Law and
legislation—United States—Juvenile literature. 4. Religion in
the public schools—Law and legislation—United States—
Juvenile literature. 5. Church and state—United States—
Juvenile literature. [1. Engel, Steven I.—Trials, litigation, etc.
2. Vitale, William J.—Trials, litigation, etc. 3. Religion in the
public schools. 4. Church and state. 5. Trials.] I. Title:
Engel versus Vitale. II. Title. III. Series.
KF228.E54 L67 2001
344.73'0796—dc21

                                                    00-009682

Table of Contents

Foreword

"The law is not an end in and of itself, nor does it provide ends. It is preeminently a means to serve what we think is right."

William J. Brennan Jr.

THE CONCEPT OF JUSTICE AND THE RULE OF LAW are hallmarks of Western civilization, manifested perhaps most visibly in widely famous and dramatic court trials. These trials include such important and memorable personages as the ancient Greek philosopher Socrates, who was accused and convicted of corrupting the minds of his society's youth in 399 B.C.; the French maiden and military leader Joan of Arc, accused and convicted of heresy against the church in 1431; to former football star O.J. Simpson, acquitted of double murder in 1995. These and other well-known and controversial trials constitute the most public, and therefore most familiar, demonstrations of a Western legal tradition that dates back through the ages. Although no one is certain when the first law code appeared or when the first formal court trials were held, Babylonian ruler Hammurabi introduced the first known law code in about 1760 B.C. It remains unclear how this code was administered, and no records of specific trials have survived. What is clear, however, is that humans have always sought to govern behavior and define actions in terms of law.

Almost all societies have made laws and prosecuted people for going against those laws, but the question of which behaviors to sanction and which to censure has always been controversial and remains in flux. Some, such as Roman orator and legislator Cicero, argue that laws are simply applications of universal standards. Cicero believed that humanity would agree on what constituted illegal behavior and that human laws were a mere extension of natural laws. "True law is right reason in agreement with nature," he wrote,

4

world-wide in scope, unchanging, everlasting. . . . We may not oppose or alter that law, we cannot abolish it, we cannot be freed from its obligations by any legislature. . . . This [natural] law does not differ for Rome and for Athens, for the present and for the future. . . . It is and will be valid for all nations and all times.

Cicero's rather optimistic view has been contradicted throughout history, however. For every law made to preserve harmony and set universal standards of behavior, another has been born of fear, prejudice, greed, desire for power, and a host of other motives. History is replete with individuals defying and fighting to change such laws—and even to topple governments that dictate such laws. Abolitionists fought against slavery, civil rights leaders fought for equal rights, millions throughout the world have fought for independence—these constitute a minimum of reasons for which people have sought to overturn laws that they believed to be wrong or unjust. In opposition to Cicero, then, many others, such as eighteenth-century English poet and philosopher William Godwin, believe humans must be constantly vigilant against bad laws. As Godwin said in 1793:

Laws we sometimes call the wisdom of our ancestors. But this is a strange imposition. It was as frequently the dictate of their passion, of timidity, jealousy, a monopolizing spirit, and a lust of power that knew no bounds. Are we not obliged perpetually to renew and remodel this misnamed wisdom of our ancestors? To correct it by a detection of their ignorance, and a censure of their intolerance?

Lucent Books' *Famous Trials* series showcases trials that exemplify both society's praiseworthy condemnation of universally unacceptable behavior, and its misguided persecution of individuals based on fear and ignorance, as well as trials that leave open the question of whether justice has been done. Each volume begins by setting the scene and providing a historical context to show how society's mores influence the trial process and the verdict.

Each book goes on to present a detailed and lively account of the trial, including liberal use of primary source material such as direct testimony, lawyers' summations, and contemporary and modern commentary. In addition, sidebars throughout the text create a broader context by presenting illuminating details about important points of law, information on key personalities, and important distinctions related to civil, federal, and criminal procedures. Thus, all of the primary and secondary source material included in both the text and the sidebars demonstrates to readers the sources and methods historians use to derive information and conclusions about such events.

Lastly, each *Famous Trials* volume includes one or more of the following comprehensive tools that motivate readers to pursue further reading and research. A timeline allows readers to see the scope of the trial at a glance, annotated bibliographies provide both sources for further research and a thorough list of works consulted, a glossary helps students with unfamiliar words and concepts, and a comprehensive index permits quick scanning of the book as a whole.

The insight of Oliver Wendell Holmes Jr., distinguished Supreme Court justice, exemplifies the theme of the *Famous Trials* series. Taken from *The Common Law*, published in 1881, Holmes remarked: "The life of the law has not been logic, it has been experience." That "experience" consists mainly in how laws are applied in society and challenged in the courts, a process resulting in differing outcomes from one generation to the next. Thus, the *Famous Trials* series encourages readers to examine trials within a broader historical and social context.

Introduction

Banning School Prayer Raises Larger Issues

IN 1962, THE U.S. Supreme Court handed down one of its most controversial decisions of the twentieth century. In the case labeled *Engel v. Vitale*, the court held that, under the U.S. Constitution's First and Fourteenth Amendments, public-school officials in New York State could not authorize the recital of a prayer during opening exercises in the schools. Government had no business allowing the saying of prayers by students in public schools, said Justice Hugo Black, speaking for the majority of the Court justices.

The public outcry against the Court's ruling was swift and loud. Perceiving an attack on religious freedom and even on religion itself, Americans from all walks of life expressed their misgivings and, in some cases, alarm. Appearing on NBC's *Tonight Show* on June 28 of that year, noted entertainers Jerry Lewis and Ed Sullivan echoed the concerns of many Americans when they suggested that the Supreme Court's decision might be part of a sinister conspiracy to destroy religious harmony in the country. A few days later the renowned Christian evangelist Billy Graham declared,

> This is another step toward the secularization [trend toward a nonreligious character] of the United States. Followed to its logical conclusion, we will have to take the chaplains out of the armed forces, prayers cannot be said in Congress, and the President cannot put his hand on the Bible when he

takes the oath of office. The framers of our Constitution meant we were to have freedom of religion, not freedom from religion.[1]

Widespread Opposition

Sharing Graham's concerns were several members of the U.S. Congress. One lawmaker proposed that funds be earmarked to pay for copies of the Bible to be given to the High Court's justices, who, in his view, needed to read it and take it to heart. In September 1962 the U.S. House of Representatives voted unanimously to display the words *In God We Trust* in plain view behind the desk of the Speaker of the House. And numerous senators introduced bills providing for constitutional amendments that would overturn the Court's ruling in *Engel v. Vitale*.

Though these and other expressions of outrage were widespread, the heat of the moment passed without any major upheavals

Reverend Billy Graham, along with many people across the United States, felt the Supreme Court's decision in Engel v. Vitale *was an attack on religious freedom.*

in the schools, society, or the Constitution itself. Though large numbers of school officials disagreed with the High Court's ruling, compliance with the law was extraordinarily widespread and uniform in most parts of the country; and new generations of schoolchildren came to see it as a matter of course that they did not pray out loud in school. Also, those legislators and others who had clamored to amend the Constitution were unable to muster the necessary political support to do so.

That did not mean that the controversy over prayer in the schools disappeared. In fact, other cases of a similar nature came before the courts, including the Supreme Court, in the years following *Engel v. Vitale*. And politicians, religious leaders, and other concerned citizens continue even today to debate the issue, some calling for prayer to be reinstated in the schools, and others insisting that the ban on prayer should remain in effect.

Perhaps even more importantly, the issue of school prayer that *Engel v. Vitale* wrestled with proved to be only the tip of the iceberg, so to speak, as it highlighted and reflected a number of larger issues and concerns in American society. Chief among these is the doctrine of separation of church and state, as enunciated in the Constitution's First Amendment, which reads, "Congress shall make no law respecting an establishment of religion, or prohibiting the free exercise thereof." Those who support the High Court's decision in *Engel v. Vitale* argue that the effort to get prayer back in the schools is only a small part of a larger effort by religious fundamentalists and others. The goal of that effort, they say, is to make the schools, government, and society in general conform to the ideas and beliefs of one particular religious faith, namely conservative Christianity. In this view, the pro–school prayer efforts are often equated with those seeking to allow the government to provide financial support for religious and alternative private schools, where religious indoctrination is legal, and to force public schools to teach creationism (the biblical version of the origins of life) instead of or on an equal basis with evolution.

Opponents of *Engel v. Vitale* often counter with the argument that they are not trying to force their religion on anyone. Rather, they simply want their children to be able to exercise their freedom of religion inside as well as outside of school. Moreover, they say, society has become much too secular, has strayed from many of the moral precepts that religion upholds, and must return to the course intended by America's founders, who were all deeply religious individuals.

Larger Issues

Among the other larger issues that *Engel v. Vitale* stirred up was the question of altering the Constitution. Many Americans feel that if they cannot get Congress and the Supreme Court to respond to their concerns about school prayer and other related issues, the answer is to amend the Constitution. Others feel that it is unwise to tamper with the Constitution too easily and too often. In their view, such a course would ultimately dilute and weaken what is arguably the greatest governmental blueprint in history.

Still other related issues are the prevalence of religious diversity and the need for religious tolerance in the United States. As City University of New York scholar Sam Duker puts it,

> In a society where there is only a minimum of diversity in religious attitudes, views, and beliefs, there is little or no difficulty in establishing satisfactory policies concerning religious activities in the schools. It is only when a diversity of views exists that the determination of such a policy presents a serious and sometimes painful problem. This problem is exacerbated [made worse] as the degree of diversity increases. Generally speaking, immigrants to the American colonies as well as to the United States have come from areas where there was little diversity in religious attitudes and beliefs. . . . To live in a society marked by extreme diversity in religious beliefs was consequently a new experience. . . . That the process of adjustment has been a difficult one, fraught with controversy, compromise, antagonism, reconciliation, emotion, and reason, is not surprising. Some adjustment can, perhaps, be facilitated by court decisions. A spirit of tolerance and understanding and above all a recognition of the reality of this diversity are, however, the most necessary ingredients.[2]

Supporters of the Engel v. Vitale *ruling feel that prayer in public schools violates the separation of church and state as outlined in the Constitution.*

Thus, aside from its elimination of prayer from American public schools, the *Engel v. Vitale* decision has brought about a larger, more profound change in society. Part of this change involves an increased awareness of the nation's cultural diversity and its laws dealing with separation of church and state. The other part is the illumination of some fundamental, deep-seated differences of opinion on these issues and the realization that a solution that will satisfy everyone, if not impossible, remains a long way off.

Chapter 1

The Establishment of Religious Practices in American Schools

E VERYONE INVOLVED IN THE *Engel v. Vitale* case and the 1962 Supreme Court decision stemming from it acknowledged that the case was directly related to the larger issue of separation of church and state. And people on both sides of the debate readily cited earlier writings and precedents having to do with that controversial issue. "The state's use of . . . prayer in its public school system," Justice Hugo Black said, for example, "breaches the constitutional wall of separation between church and state."[3] Since America's founders conceived and wrote the Constitution, including its provisions against the mixing of government and religion, their opinions were and remain of special interest to those involved in the debate. In particular, the views of James Madison and Thomas Jefferson, who were heavily involved in framing pivotal documents like the Declaration of Independence and the Constitution, are of continuing relevance.

Therefore, to understand and appreciate why *Engel v. Vitale* was so important and why the debate over school prayer still rages in American society, it is necessary to examine how the relationship between religion and government was perceived by the nation's founders and the generations of Americans who followed them. For it is in the first century or so of the nation's history that the roots of the institutions of church and state first became intertwined. Over time, their relationship grew and established a long-standing history of religious practices in public institutions. And these traditions still linger, despite Supreme Court efforts to separate church from state.

Religion's Hold over Colonial America

One of the reasons people originally immigrated to America was to avoid religious persecution in England. However, religious conflict and persecution followed them across the Atlantic Ocean as the settlers sought the freedom to express their religious beliefs in any way that they desired. They also sought freedom from the one established church, which had influence over all citizens, commerce, and politics. Yet despite their intentions, early Americans could not escape the tension caused by the existence and interaction of

JEFFERSON ON THE SEPARATION OF CHURCH AND STATE

One of the earliest statements about the issue of separation of church and state was this letter (as it appears in David Barton's *Original Intent*), written by Thomas Jefferson on January 1, 1802, and sent to the Danbury Baptist Association. The Baptists had earlier expressed concerns over the First Amendment, which they feared might restrict religious rights.

> Believing with you that religion is a matter that lies solely between man and his God; that he owes account to none other for his faith or his worship; that the legislative powers of the Government reach action only, and not opinions, I contemplate with sovereign reverence that act of the whole American people which declared that their legislature should "make no law respecting an establishment of religion or prohibiting the free exercise thereof," thus building a wall of separation between church and State. Adhering to this expression of the supreme will of the nation in behalf of the rights of conscience, I shall see with sincere satisfaction the progress of those sentiments which tend to restore to man all his natural rights, convinced [that] he has no natural right in opposition to his social duties.

Puritans, seen here on their way to worship in 1667, came to America to obtain religious freedom.

different religious beliefs and practices. And they ultimately established colonies where those who shared a predominant belief and manner of worship became dominant.

The Puritans, for example, established the Massachusetts Bay Colony as a theocratic state (a government whose officials believe they are guided by God) in which Catholics, Quakers, and others were regarded as dangerous dissidents and were subject to the death penalty. In turn, the Catholics who founded Maryland persecuted Protestants. Rhode Island, on the other hand, believed that all religions should be allowed to coexist and flourish together.

By 1775 nine colonies had arrangements that established a single church that occupied a privileged position within the colony, was vested with certain powers denied to others, and was supported by the public treasury. Massachusetts, Connecticut, and New Hampshire, for instance, established themselves as Congregationalist. In the South, by contrast, the colonists were mostly Episcopal; meanwhile, the residents of New York supported Protestant clergymen. Gradually, some influential members of these separate colonial societies came to recognize that mistrust and bickering over their religious differences would inevitably lead to warfare and destruction. And as a solution, some advocated the concept of separating church and state, which might ensure religious freedom for all.

But reducing the hold that colonial churches had on society was not an easy task. Religious belief and practice had become almost irrevocably entangled with public and private life, commerce, and politics. This relationship had come to be called "excessive entanglement," and most people saw that religion could not be completely disentangled from everyday life. Moreover, no one wanted to go that far since nearly all of the colonist were devout Christians. Even just before and during the American Revolution, when the founding fathers actively tried to keep church and state separate, they did not eliminate or ban common, highly ingrained religious customs. For example, appeals for God to help them in their deliberations, days of prayer and fasting, and other religious observances were common among members of the Continental Congresses. In fact, among the first items of business in the First Continental Congress in 1774 was to appoint a chaplain and open the meeting with a prayer. (Congress continues to observe this practice today.)

Fear of Government-Imposed Religion

Still, by the end of the revolution, a number of American political leaders, James Madison and Thomas Jefferson prominent among them, had become more convinced than ever that religion should have no significant influence in governmental affairs. The danger these men saw was the possibility that a ruler (or ruling group) might impose his (or their) personal religious beliefs on an unwilling populace. It would be better, the political leaders reasoned, to allow everyone to believe and worship as they pleased without governmental interference; and the only certain way to accomplish this goal was to make sure that government did not officially profess or support any specific religious system.

With these ideas in mind, and with the support of Madison and others, in 1786 Jefferson helped enact the Virginia Statute of

Despite its efforts to separate church and state, the First Continental Congress (here being addressed by Patrick Henry) continued to practice many religious customs.

Religious Freedom. This act established a doctrine of religious tolerance and forbade the use of general tax funds to support a single church. In guaranteeing religious liberty and condemning the use of political power by an established religion, this law was a direct precursor to the First Amendment of the Constitution, which forbids Congress from establishing a religion. "The impious [lacking proper respect] presumption of legislature and ruler," Jefferson wrote in the statute,

> who, being themselves but fallible [able to make mistakes] and uninspired men, have assumed dominion [power] over the faith of others, setting up their own opinions and modes of thinking as the only true and infallible [ones] . . . hath established and maintained false religions over the greatest part of the world and through all time. . . . [This] tends also to corrupt the principles of that very religion it is meant to encourage. . . . [Therefore] the [religious] opinions of men are not the object of civil government.[4]

Meanwhile, even though the established state churches had been disestablished, religious belief and worship continued in small but numerous ways to affect the thinking and policies of lawmakers and the conduct of federal, state, and local governments. Church property was usually tax exempt; under what were known as "blue laws," stores were required to close on Sundays; Christmas and Thanksgiving were federal holidays; and state legislatures began each day's session with a prayer, to name only a few examples. Indeed, Justice William O. Douglas correctly observed in a 1952 Supreme Court opinion, "We are a

Some religious customs, such as Thanksgiving, are so deeply ingrained in American culture and history that the federal government continues to recognize them today.

How Did Jefferson Feel About Religion?

Although thoroughly educated in Protestant theology, Jefferson considered himself a "Deist," one whose beliefs are free of creed and dogma yet express the general belief in a divine creator. Those who adhere to Deism believe that God is to be found through reason rather than revelation, that God created the world and afterwards refrained from interfering with its working, and that heaven and hell are of humanity's own making.

Because Jefferson rejected religious dogma, at times—especially in his later years when he no longer feared political repercussions—he made strongly worded negative statements about well-known religious leaders. Some people incorrectly interpreted these statements as antireligious expressions. In his famous *Notes on Virginia*, for example, Jefferson comments on his own religious openmindedness by saying, "It does me no injury for my neighbor to say there are twenty gods or no gods. It neither picks my pocket nor breaks my leg." Many New England clergymen found this remark offensive and suggested that it showed that Jefferson was an atheist and heretic. Jefferson countered that such people knew nothing about his religious opinions, and he wrote a brief essay in which he praised both Jesus Christ and the Greek philosopher Socrates as great proponents of human values.

religious people whose institutions presuppose a Supreme Being."[5] Because of this presupposition, Americans continued to observe various religious customs in politics, business, and schools.

It was not until the mid-twentieth century that anyone seriously challenged the constitutionality of the relationship between federally and state-funded projects and religion. And even then, this issue was contested only in the public schools. The *Engel v. Vitale* case determined that institutions working with children needed to protect them from what Jefferson had feared—the imposition of compulsory religious expression. Furthermore, the case established that children should be free from the influence of churches and beliefs that their families might not share. Otherwise, schools could be seen as supporting, through government funds, not only Judeo-Christian beliefs but also a state-funded religion.

School Prayer and Bible Readings in Early America

The *Engel v. Vitale* case was, of course, preceded by a long history of religious practices in American public schools. Colonial schools, predominantly attended by Protestants and Catholics, included not only saying prayers each day but also Bible reading and instruction as a way of forming the basis of moral and intellectual development. This set a precedent for the later introduction of religious concepts in American education.

In 1787 Congress ratified the Northwest Ordinance, which regulated the settlement of land between the Ohio and Mississippi Rivers. The ordinance also created public-school districts within each plot of land. These districts were not supported by Catholic or Protestant Church funds, but rather through state taxes. On the other hand, the ordinance established prayer and moral development as a part of every student's school instruction. Children often learned to read using the Bible as a textbook, and instruction in morality was derived primarily from biblical proverbs.

In early American schools (such as this one in New Canaan, Connecticut), students not only said prayers each day but also studied the Bible.

JAMES MADISON AND THE WORDING OF THE ESTABLISHMENT CLAUSE

To prevent future misunderstandings of their religious views, America's founders were careful about the wording they chose in composing official legal documents. For instance, when James Madison arrived at the First Continental Congress with his initial proposal for the First Amendment, one of the provisions read that "the civil rights of none shall be abridged on account of religious belief or worship, nor shall any national religion be established." Madison argued that the insertion of the word *national* before the word *religion* in the committee version would satisfy the minds of those who were critical of the amendment. He also believed that people feared that one religious sect might attain preeminence, or two might combine and establish a religion to which they would compel others to conform. He thought the word *national* would focus the provision directly on the situation it was intended to prevent— the formation of a state-sponsored, national religion.

Madison's original language in what became known as the establishment clause did not last long. It was sent to a select committee of the House, which, without explanation, changed it to read that "no religion shall be established by law." It was further changed by the Committee of the Whole until it read, "Congress shall make no laws touching religion." This sentence, however, would have forbidden Congress from making laws having anything to do with religion and was far broader than Madison's version and broader even than the scope of the establishment clause as it now reads.

Just two years after the Northwest Ordinance passed, the U.S. Constitution was drafted; ironically, its First Amendment, which would later become a basis for the Supreme Court's *Engel v. Vitale* decision, at first was interpreted as strongly encouraging prayer and other religious practices in schools. The First Amendment reads, "Congress shall make no law respecting the establishment of religion, or prohibiting the free exercise thereof; or abridging the freedom of speech, or of the press; or the right of the people peaceably to assemble, and to petition the Government for a redress of grievances." In the years immediately following the Constitution's ratification, almost all public-school officials interpreted the phrase "free exercise" of religion to mean that children and adults were free to continue the practice of prayer and Bible reading or instruction during classroom hours and activities. Moreover, during nonschool hours many public schools were also used as churches and as places for people to assemble freely for religious activity without the fear that any other group or the government would interfere.

Is Forbidding Religion in Schools Anti-Christian?

Though the free exercise clause of the First Amendment was long taken to encourage religious practices in the schools, another part of the amendment seemed to discourage such practices. This is the so-called establishment clause, which says that the government cannot make any law establishing any sort of officially sanctioned religion.

For a long time, however, the establishment clause did not prove to be a roadblock to prayer, the teaching of biblical morality, or other kinds of religious practices in schools. As early as the mid-1840s, the Supreme Court was asked to hear a case known as *Vidal v. Girard's Executors*, which dealt with the validity of attempting to impart Christian morals to all students in a school. The case involved the will left by a Frenchman named Stephen Girard, who had arrived in America before the American Revolution. When Girard died in 1831, he left his property,

which was valued at $7 million, to the city of Philadelphia, provided that certain conditions were met. The main condition was that the city had to build an orphanage with a school attached, and that there could be no religious practices or indoctrination of any kind in this school. Girard required that "no

Stephen Girard's attempt to exclude religion from a government-run school was unprecedented.

ecclesiastic [priest], missionary, or minister of any sect whatsoever, shall ever hold or exercise any station or duty whatever in said college."[6]

In response to this unprecedented attempt to exclude religion from a government-run school, Girard's heirs (the Executors) filed suit, saying that such an arrangement was "anti-Christian and therefore repugnant [repulsive or incompatible] to the law."[7] The city's lawyers, who obviously wanted Philadelphia to get Girard's money, defended the validity of his will.

The case eventually went to the Supreme Court. In 1844 Justice Joseph Story delivered the court's unanimous decision, which struck a sort of compromise. On the one hand, the justices said, Philadelphia could receive Girard's estate. But on the other, Christian religious practices, such as daily prayers, bible reading, and the teaching of Biblical morality, should not and could not be excluded from the school. "Christianity," said Story,

> is not to be maliciously and openly reviled and blasphemed against to the annoyance of believers or the injury of the public. . . . Why may not the Bible, and especially the New Testament, without note or comment, be read [in the school] . . . as a divine revelation . . . its general precepts expounded, its evidences explained and its glorious principles of morality inculcated [indoctrinated into the students]? . . . Where can the purest principles of morality be learned so clearly or so perfectly as from the New Testament?[8]

The major outcome of this important case, therefore, was that the Supreme Court emphatically allowed religious practices in government-sponsored schools, including indoctrination in biblical morality. The justices did not view their decision as an infringement of the doctrine on separation of church and state, perhaps because at the time that doctrine was still widely thought to apply mainly to political institutions such as legislatures and government offices, and not to educational institutions.

A Complex Religious-Educational Environment

This integration of religious practices into school curricula was maintained in U.S. public schools, in one form or another, well into the 1900s. A 1956 survey by the National Education Association showed that at least six states—Arkansas, Delaware, Kansas, Maine, New Jersey, and North Dakota—authorized the recitation of the Lord's Prayer or the reading of the Ten Commandments or other biblical quotations during a typical school day. The study further found that about half of the states had laws requiring or permitting Bible reading in public schools. In 1956 one Tennessee court even upheld what it called "simple ceremonies," activities that combined Bible reading with prayer and the singing of Christian hymns. Furthermore, a 1960 survey found that 42 percent of the school districts in the continental United States reported daily Bible reading in their schools, and 50 percent had some sort of daily homeroom devotional exercises, almost always including prayer.

By the 1960s, religious practices in schools and the state laws governing them varied widely across the country.

These sorts of religious practices in schools were not uniform from a geographic and demographic standpoint, however. In other words, in some parts of the country they were the rule while in other parts they were the exception, as local school districts set their individual standards. For instance, another early 1960s' survey of elementary-school religious practices revealed that different religious practices and trends were found in different parts of the country. The survey showed, for example, that 80 percent of teachers in the South had Bible reading in their classrooms, and 87 percent of their students recited morning prayers in their classes. In the Eastern states, 62 percent of teachers read the Bible in class, and 83 percent led their students in prayer. In the Midwest, though, the numbers differed dramatically; there, only 28 percent of teachers read from the Bible, and just 38 percent of students prayed in class. And in the West, 14 percent of teachers read from the Bible, and 14 percent of students recited morning prayers in class. Moreover, eleven states (mostly in the West) had laws prohibiting Bible reading; eleven others (mostly in the South) had laws requiring Bible reading; and twenty-six other states had laws that permitted, but did not require, the practice. These markedly differing statistics regarding religious practices in the schools reflected a distinct polarization in public opinion on the issue. And this would show up later in differing degrees of acceptance or rejection of the 1962 *Engel v. Vitale* High Court decision.

This complex and highly diverse religious-educational environment was bound to present a deep-seated emotional challenge, as well as a constitutional challenge, for any judge faced with deciding a case on school prayer or any other school-based religious practice. Certainly, no judge wanted to be the one to ignite public controversy by removing all religious practices from public schools. However, as the *Engel v. Vitale* case finally made its way through the courts, several state judges and eventually the Supreme Court justices were forced to answer the difficult question of whether religion had a place in America's public education system.

Chapter 2

The New York Courts Consider a Protest Against School Prayer

THE SERIES OF INCIDENTS leading up to the now famous *Engel v. Vitale* case began in 1958 on Long Island, New York. That year, the New York State Board of Regents, the body that governed the state's public-school system, decided that it wanted to set a standard for moral and spiritual training in that system. Various religious practices, including prayer and Bible reading, already were in place in many New York schools. But they were not at all uniform, and the Board of Regents felt that some measure of uniformity was needed to ensure that all students in the state received some kind of moral instruction. As part of this effort, the board drafted a short prayer and recommended that it be recited in opening exercises in classrooms throughout the state. The prayer read, "Almighty God, we acknowledge our dependence upon Thee, and we beg Thy blessings upon us, our parents, our teachers and our Country."[9]

Dutifully following this recommendation, about 10 percent of the school districts in the state began using the prayer, and many others seriously considered doing so. One district that moved quickly to adopt the regents' prayer was the Union Free District No. 9 in Long Island's town of New Hyde Park, where the local board of education ordered that the prayer be incorporated into every school's curriculum. In these and the other participating

Nearly twenty years after the Engel *case first came to light, voluntary prayer still existed in American public schools like this one in Boston, Massachusetts.*

New York schools, few, if any, of the school officials considered the issue of whether the state was obligating the children to say the prayer. This was because the Board of Regents' recommendation had made some provisions for nonparticipation by any children who did not wish to recite the prayer.

But a small group of New Hyde Park citizens viewed these provisions as inadequate. Five sets of parents, who had a total of eleven children in the district's schools, felt that the state was indeed obligating students to take part in prayers—specifically Christian ones. Two of the families were Jewish; one was Unitarian; one belonged to the Society of Ethical Culture (a religious group that advocates moral behavior without adhering to a specific religious creed); and the members of the fifth family were, according to the father, Lawrence Roth, nonbelievers. Regardless of their specific beliefs, each family's objection was the same: that the Board of Regents was violating the establishment clause of the First Amendment.

Concerns About Government-Sponsored Religion

Lawrence Roth's reaction to the Board of Regents' policy was similar to those of the other parents involved. When Roth's two sons came home one day in 1958 and told him about the new prayer being recited at school, he was disturbed. In his mind, the prayer was a way of imposing a conformity of religious belief and worship on his children; moreover, the move had clearly been instigated by the government since the Board of Regents was a governmental agency created by the state's constitution and it directly supervised the state's school districts. Thus, Roth reasoned, the government, in the guise of the school board, was imposing a set of religious beliefs on his children.

For these reasons, Roth was determined to eliminate the prayer from the classroom. He solicited the views of other parents in the district and found that several agreed with his view that the state should be neutral in religious matters and not impose religious beliefs or practices on anyone. In particular, these parents agreed, the state should exclude the practice of prayer from the classroom.

In the minds of these parents, the first logical step in dealing with the problem was to lodge a complaint with the local school board. For a number of months during 1958, school board meetings were a forum for the voices of angry parents. Speaking out in these

"My teacher caught me praying!"

© Gene Myers.

THE HIGH COURT IS ACCUSED OF STIFLING FREEDOM OF EXPRESSION

This description of the second notable mention of the phrase "separation of church and state" (after Jefferson's letter to the Baptists) is from "School Prayer and Religious Liberty: A Constitutional Perspective," published on August 7, 1997, by Concerned Women for America. Note that the organization is critical of what it sees as attempts by the Supreme Court to use the establishment clause to stifle freedom of religious expression.

[The mention came] in the 1947 Supreme Court case, *Everson v. Board of Education*. The plaintiff argued that the New Jersey law that reimbursed parents for the cost of bus transportation—to public and religious schools—violated the establishment clause of the First Amendment. The Supreme Court said that it did not. In the majority opinion, however, Justice Black used language [designed] to set the stage for damaging rulings in the future [that is, supposedly damaging to the freedom of expression]. He wrote that the Establishment Clause created a "complete separation between the state and religion." Jefferson's letter was written 10 years after the ratification of the First Amendment, yet Black relied upon his own interpretation of Jefferson's words, rather than on the text of the First Amendment, to set the *Everson* precedent for future rulings. Twentieth century courts, based predominately on Jefferson's letter and on the precedent created by Justice Black in *Everson v. Board of Education,* have argued that the Constitution intended to separate all religious expression from public life. Yet that ignores the textual history and the original intent of the author of these religion clauses, James Madison. It also ignores the broad, historical context. The men who hammered out each section of the Constitution also believed in the importance of daily prayer. The Establishment Clause has often been misinterpreted to mean that any link to religion is "establishing" religion. One of the causes of this is a simple alteration of the wording in the First Amendment. The clause reads, "Congress shall make no law regarding an establishment of religion." It does not read, "Congress shall make no law regarding the establishment of religion," as it is often misquoted. If the article is read as "the," then it refers to establishment of all religion in general. If the article is "an," then it clearly refers to a specific religion or denomination— an interpretation backed up by historic records. Realizing that the amendment uses the word "an" helps elucidate the meaning of the Framers. So, rather than attempting to separate themselves from religious belief and expression, the Framers were trying to keep one denomination from being favored over another.

meetings, Roth and others requested that the practice of opening the school day with a prayer cease. But after much debate, the board members decided that the prayer would continue in the New Hyde Park schools. Children were not required to pray, they said. Children who did not wish to take part, said the board, could stand or sit silently or even leave the room if a parent wrote a note excusing the child from the classroom during the opening exercises. Moreover, the board reasoned that the prayer had been drafted with the utmost care to be ecumenical in nature—that is, it included general phrases that did not single out or endorse the beliefs of Protestants, Catholics, Jews, or any other religious group.

The Decision to File Suit

Roth and the other parents who had protested to the local school board were dissatisfied with the board's decision and decided they had no other choice but to take their case to court. To help drum up support for such an effort, they placed an ad in the local newspapers calling for other parents to join in a legal challenge to the prayer recitals. Although they received about fifty positive responses, by December 1958 most of these interested parents dropped out of the suit. Some cited personal reasons, but others admitted that social pressure had forced them to quit. Indeed, after the community learned about the suit, many of those who had expressed an interest in joining the action found themselves the targets of a campaign of hate and abuse. Some received telephoned threats, and others found obscene materials in their mail, all apparently designed to frighten them out of pursuing the lawsuit.

In January 1959 Roth and his wife and the four other sets of parents who still wanted to pursue legal action finally took their case to the Supreme Court of Nassau County. They were aided by the American Civil Liberties Union (ACLU), which had heard about the case and stepped forward to assist by providing professional legal representation.

While waiting for the county court to hear the case, some of the children of the parents bringing the suit found that attending school had become a constant battle against harassment. Those who chose not to take part in the prayer recital had to endure the verbal abuse of many of their classmates. Lenore Lyons, the mother of four of the children involved in the case, stated that her children suffered taunts and threats simply because they remained seated and silent during the prayer. Meanwhile, the suing parents themselves continued to endure abuse, via telephone calls and letters, at the hands of persons who saw the legal action as anti-Christian.

THE ACLU EXPLAINS ITS POSITION ON CHURCH-STATE SEPARATION

The American Civil Liberties Union (ACLU) published this statement, from its 1996 document "Religious Liberty," to explain why it strongly supports all efforts to keep church and state separate.

With more than 1,500 different religious bodies, and 360,000 churches, mosques and synagogues, the U.S. is the most religiously diverse, and one of the most devout countries in the world. Moreover, we enjoy unparalleled religious liberty, and sectarian strife is relatively rare. Today, however, religious extremists are attempting to impose their beliefs and practices on everyone else by enlisting the government's support and aid. These efforts, if successful, will threaten each individual's right to worship, or not worship, as he or she pleases. Some people mistakenly believe that separation of church and state implies hostility to religion. But in fact, the opposite is true. The Constitution's framers understood very well that religious liberty can flourish only if the government leaves religion alone. The free exercise clause of the First Amendment guarantees the right to practice one's religion free of government interference. The establishment clause requires the separation of church and state. Combined, they ensure religious liberty.

Trinity Church in Boston, Massachusetts is just one of 360,000 churches, mosques, and synagogues in the United States.

Even though students in the New Hyde Park schools were not required to pray and could be excused from the classroom during the prayer, many suffered harassment from classmates for not participating.

The First Judge Sides with the School Board

When the county court heard the case later in 1959, the plaintiffs' attorneys argued that reciting the prayer constituted a violation of the First Amendment. The lawyers also stated that the use of an official prayer in the public schools was contrary to the beliefs and religious practices of their clients and their children. Defending the use of the prayer, attorneys for the school board contended that the district's religious heritage and traditions needed to be maintained as the foundation for moral and spiritual development. They further contended that schools had a mandate to reinforce moral development during the school day. They also maintained that the prayer was merely "recommended" for use and that principals, teachers, and students were not being compelled to recite the prayers every morning.

After hearing both sides of the issue, the court rendered its verdict. There was nothing wrong with the prayer recitals, said the court, as long as they were not compulsory for the students. The judge declared that a "teacher might open his school with prayer provided he does not encroach upon the hours allotted to instruction and provided that the attendance of scholars [students] was not exacted [required] as a matter of school discipline."[10] In support of this opinion, the judge cited a 1912 report published by the New York State Department of Education, which listed several prior state legal rulings about prayer in the classroom. None of these rulings, he said, had found such prayers objectionable. As further precedent, the judge quoted an 1839 statement by a New York school superintendent, which said, in part,

> Both parties have rights, the one to bring up their children in the practice of publicly thanking their Creator for His protection and invoking His Blessing; [and] the other in declining in behalf of their children the religious services of any person in whose creed they may not concur or for other reasons satisfactory to themselves. . . . Those who desire that their children engage in public prayer have no right to compel other children to unite in the exercise, against the wishes of their parents. Nor have those who object to this time, place, or manner of praying . . . a right to deprive the other class of the opportunity of habituating their child to what they conceive as imperious [urgent and pressing] duty.[11]

Based on this and other similar arguments, the judge made it clear that, while the prayer exercise could continue, those who objected to it must be entirely free of any compulsion to take part; and that schools must institute safeguards against any embarrassments or pressures that might make the students feel an obligation to join in the prayer.

As for the issue of whether the prayer infringed on the establishment clause of the First Amendment, the judge stated,

> The recognition of prayer is an integral part of our national heritage, one that, therefore, the (establishment) clause cannot have been intended to outlaw the practice in schools any more than for the rest of public life; that is, that prayer in the schools is permissible not as a means of teaching "spiritual values" but because traditionally, and partic-

ularly at the time of the adoption of the First Amendment
. . . this was the accepted practice.[12]

The Appellate Court's Decision

The parents who had brought the suit were not willing to let the
matter rest with the County Court's decision against them. Two of
the parents, Steven Engel and Daniel Lichtenstein, each of whom
had two children in the schools, now stepped forward and took the
lead in appealing the case to a higher court—the New York State
Appellate Division. In October 1960 that court upheld the county
court's ruling. So Engel and the others appealed once more, this
time to the state's highest appellate court—the New York Court of
Appeals.

The parents were again disappointed when, in July 1961, the
New York Court of Appeals upheld the decisions of the lower state
courts to allow the school prayer to stand in New Hyde Park. Of
the seven judges who reviewed the case, five voted in favor of
upholding the prior court decisions and two dissented. Chief Judge
Desmond spoke for the majority when he said that the argument
of the appeal seemed to be

that the saying of the "Regents' prayer" as a daily school exercise is a form of State-sponsored religious education and is accordingly an unconstitutional "establishment" of religion. . . . But it is not "religious education," nor is it the practice of or establishment of religion in any reasonable meaning of those phrases. Saying this simple prayer may be, according to the broadest possible dictionary definition, an act of "religion," but when the founding fathers prohibited an "establishment of religion," they were referring to official adoption of, or favor to, one or more [religious] sects. They could not have meant to prohibit mere professions of belief in God for, if that were so, they themselves were in many ways violating their rule when and after they adopted it. . . . It is an indisputable and historically provable fact that belief and trust in a Creator has always been regarded as an integral and inseparable part of the fabric of our fundamental institutions.[13]

Here, Judge Desmond concurred with the judge of the county court, both men arguing in effect that school prayer was valid partly because it was a cherished tradition. To this, one of Desmond's concurring colleagues, Judge Froessel, added the argument that other religious references and practices were ingrained and accepted in the American system. "The challenged recitation [of prayer] follows the pledge of allegiance," he stated,

> which itself refers to God. School children are permitted to sing "America," the fourth stanza of which is indeed a prayer, invoking the protection of "God," "Author of Liberty." The preamble to our state constitution, which is taught in our public schools, provides: "We the People of the State of New York, grateful to the Almighty God for our Freedom." . . . To say that such references . . . may be sanctioned by public officials everywhere but in the public school room defies understanding.[14]

Disagreeing with his colleagues, one of the dissenters, Judge Dye, wasted little time with arguments about tradition and instead focused on the issue of separation of church and state. He admit-

The debate over prayer in school also put into question the pledge of allegiance, a cherished tradition which includes a reference to God.

ted that Americans were and undoubtedly remain a deeply religious people. Yet there is a clearly defined line of separation between the government and religion, "which may not be overstepped in the slightest degree in favor of either the church or the State." According to Dye, the regents' prayer should not be allowed, therefore, because it was clearly "a form of State-sponsored religious education." Dye concluded by insisting that

> the inculcation of religion is a matter for the family and the church. In sponsoring a religious program, the State enters a field which it has been thought best to leave to the church alone. . . . [As part of a religious program, school prayer] gives the State a direct supervision and influence that overstep the line marking the division between church and State and cannot help but lead to a gradual erosion of the mighty bulwark [defensive wall] erected by the First Amendment.[15]

To Take the Final Step?

Now that the county court, the appellate division, and the New York Court of Appeals had all upheld the local school board's use of the prayer in the classroom, just one other legal forum remained—the U.S. Supreme Court, which had the power to overturn all of the previous decisions. But would the High Court echo the words of Judge Dye, who felt that the ties between church and state in the schools, however traditional, should be severed? It seemed to Engel and his fellow petitioners that they had put in a great deal of time and effort and that it was worth taking the final step in the legal process.

To that end, Engel and the others decided to engage the services of attorney William J. Butler, who soon secured the assistance of Leo Pfeffer of the Synagogue Council of America as well as lawyers from the ACLU. Butler and his legal team alleged that the daily use of the prayer failed to protect the rights of both believers and nonbelievers. They also claimed that official prayers composed by any governmental entity, including a school, constituted governmental establishment of religion; and this, they said, was a clear violation of the Constitution. By wording the case in this manner, Engel's attorneys established an argument that would automatically be eligible for review by the Supreme Court. The question was whether the Court would actually agree to hear the case, for it was not obligated to do so.

Chapter 3

The Supreme Court
Hears the Case

AFTER THE NEW HYDE PARK families petitioned the Supreme Court to hear their case, they waited anxiously for news. They were aware that the Supreme Court justices receive hundreds and sometimes thousands of requests each year to hear cases and that they typically decline to hear about 98 percent of the cases that come before them. The families knew that if the Court declined to hear their case, the decision by the Court of Appeals would stand and there would be no further recourse.

William J. Butler advised his clients in detail about what to expect. If the justices did decide to hear the case, he said, the litigants would no longer be called plaintiffs and defendants. The people bringing a case before the Supreme Court are referred to as the petitioners, and their opponents are called the respondents. As the lead attorney for the petitioners, Butler explained, he would have three months to prepare his arguments, which he would set down in a document called a brief. He would file the brief with the High Court, and the justices would review its contents. Then, on an appointed date, he and the lead attorney for the respondents would appear in the main chamber of the Supreme Court and present their oral arguments. This would be a question-and-answer session lasting from one to three hours, in which the justices could each grill the lawyers in an attempt to explore the issues of the case in more detail. Following oral arguments, the justices would deliberate over a period of some months and, when ready, would deliver their decision.

HOW THE SUPREME COURT CHOOSES CASES

Many people are puzzled about how the justices of the Supreme Court actually go about deciding which cases they will hear and which they will reject. The fact is that the process of acceptance and rejection of cases goes on behind closed doors, and the justices do not have to explain the reasons for their choices. "Whether or not a case is accepted strikes me as a rather subjective decision, made up in part of intuition and in part of legal judgment," Justice William Rehnquist wrote in his 1997 book *The Supreme Court: How It Was, How It Is*. Important factors in the acceptance process apparently include whether the Court can clarify contradicting decisions from lower courts, whether the lower court decisions conflict with previous Supreme Court decisions, and how much influence the Supreme Court decision would have on the American public. The justices do not automatically take on all cases posing significant public issues, however. Before voting which cases to take, the potential cases are first reviewed by staff law clerks, usually recent graduates from law schools. About seven thousand annual petitions flood into the Supreme Court and the law clerks select those petitions that they believe the justices would want to review. Four of the nine justices must then vote in favor of reviewing a case and hearing oral arguments. With the clerks' memos in hand, behind closed conference doors, the justices discuss petitions and vote aloud by seniority, starting with the chief justice.

The petitioners in *Engel v. Vitale* were relieved and delighted when the news they had been hoping for finally came on December 4, 1961. The Supreme Court had decided to hear their case and had scheduled oral arguments for April 4, 1962. Butler, who had already been working on his arguments, began preparing his brief in earnest.

On the morning of April 4, 1962, the petitioners, respondents, their attorneys, and numerous spectators filed into the main chamber of the Supreme Court and awaited the entrance of the nine justices. Among those in the courtroom were nineteen state attorneys general, who had filed their own briefs to support the constitutionality of the prayer and continue the tradition of prayer in schools. Their position would be argued by attorneys Bertram B. Daiker and Porter R. Chandler, who represented the respondents (the New Hyde Park district school board and sixteen local families who wanted to see the prayer continue).

The ACLU and various Jewish and other organizations had also filed briefs, theirs denying the constitutionality of the prayer and declaring that the government-sanctioned activity of promoting religion was barred by the First Amendment. Butler, the lawyer for the petitioners, would argue their position. Meanwhile, hundreds of interested citizens gathered outside to demonstrate, some of them supporters and others opponents of the petitioners' position.

The Petitioners' Arguments

When the nine justices entered and took their seats, the oral arguments began. Butler spoke first. His opening argument focused on the doctrine of separation of church and state. The introduction of the prayer into New Hyde Park classrooms, he said, "raises, in our opinion, grave constitutional problems. . . . It is our thesis [that this case] involves an attempt by the state to introduce religious education and observance into the public school system of our nation."

The United States Supreme Court building. The petitioners in Engel v. Vitale *were delighted when the Supreme Court justices agreed to hear their case in April 1962.*

The question at hand, Butler continued, was "to what extent can the state participate in the religious training of our youth?"[16] His answer was that the state should not assume such a role. The regents' prayer was a religious activity, he said, a fact that the school board had not attempted to deny; as a religious activity, it violated the guarantee of religious freedom inherent in the First Amendment.

Second, Butler argued, the prayer in question was not voluntary, as the respondents had so emphatically claimed. True, he admitted, the lower courts had stated that children were permitted to choose not to take part in the prayer. They could either leave the room or remain seated and silent while their classmates stood and prayed. Yet, since the time that the school board had adopted the prayer in 1958, Butler said, only one child had sought to be excused from it. The reason for this was that any child who dared to refrain from the exercise was subjected to strenuous peer pressure, as the child's classmates berated and teased him or her for being different. Butler argued that the children so disliked being different and risking rejection by their classmates that the prayer was in reality compulsory, despite the theoretical possibility of being excused. "Would a parent ask his child to leave the classroom and label himself a nonconformist?"[17] he asked.

The third point Butler made was that when the government sponsors a religious practice, either in a school or anywhere else, it makes the same mistake that European governments did in the sixteenth and seventeenth centuries. Feeling oppressed by their rulers, many Europeans had fled to the Americas to seek religious freedom. America's founders had recognized this fact and carefully crafted the Constitution to guarantee that people would be free from government interference in their beliefs. Therefore, said Butler, a school prayer created and imposed by the government went against the spirit of those who founded the nation. Specifically, he declared, returning to the issue of separation of church and state, the practice of reciting the regents' prayer "rejects the belief on which the founding fathers built our national government—a belief in the necessity for absolute separation of church and state. It threatens not merely to breach the wall of separation, but to undermine it completely."[18]

The petitioners in Engel v. Vitale *argued that school prayer went against the spirit of America's founders who fled Europe to seek religious freedom.*

The next argument offered by the petitioners was that it was also unconstitutional for the teachers themselves to be involved in administering the prayer. This, Butler said, was because the teachers were public employees paid by the local taxpayers. They were therefore government employees and, according to the doctrine of separation of church and state inherent in the First Amendment, they had no business administering a prayer in the course of their professional duties. Moreover, he stated, such teachers were authority figures whose own beliefs and conduct had an influence

THE HIGH COURT: THE NATION'S CONSCIENCE?

This brief but powerful statement appeared in the July 9, 1962, edition of the *New Republic* when the Supreme Court was under a great deal of fire for its ruling in favor of the petitioners in the *Engel v. Vitale* case. The statement was intended to explain to the public why the High Court must sometimes make decisions that are unpopular with a majority of Americans.

To many, of course, the prudence of a Court decision to entertain a case is not even a legitimate issue. They see the law as an absolute and the Court as its prophet. If a practice is unconstitutional, the Court must forbid it. Even if this may undermine the position of the Court, that is the risk that must be run. In cases where some substantial issue is at stake where the Court is protecting an unpopular minority from an angry majority, such absolutism is certainly in order. The Court is the conscience of the nation.

on the students. When a teacher administered the prayer in class, all of the students heard a resounding message that he or she advocated certain religious beliefs.

Finally, Butler tackled the issue of the government's sponsorship or support of Christian versus non-Christian beliefs. First, the prayer in question was clearly a Christian one, despite the respondents' claim that it expressed general religious sentiments acceptable to everyone. What about non-Christians, agnostics (those who are unsure, undecided, or unconcerned about religious matters and the existence of God), atheists (those who adamantly believe that God does not exist), and others?, Butler asked. They might well find the term *Almighty God* contained in the prayer to be offensive. Also, even if some students were excused from saying the prayer, it was an infringement on their constitutional rights to force them to stand and listen to a religious statement markedly contrary to their own beliefs.

Butler Clarifies His Position

During his presentation of these arguments, some of the justices interrupted Butler to ask for clarification or to comment on various points he had made. One of the most spirited and memorable exchanges occurred when Butler noted,

There is no dispute . . . [between myself and my opponents] as to . . . the purpose of this prayer [being said each day in the public schools]. . . . [It is] to inculcate into the children a love of God and respect for the Almighty . . . and to bring the children into a religious activity which in the long run . . . will preserve the religious and even Christian heritage of our society.[19]

"Is that bad?"[20] Justice John M. Harlan asked. His tone betrayed that he was somewhat surprised and befuddled by Butler's statement.

Realizing that he might have made it sound as if he were condemning religion itself, Butler was quick to clarify his position. "I want to make it absolutely clear," he said, raising his voice and thumping his hand on the lectern for emphasis,

that I do not come here as an antagonist of religion, that my clients are deeply religious people, that we come here in the firm belief that the best safety for religion in the United States and [for] freedom of religion is to keep religion out of our public life. . . . I say that prayer is good; my clients say prayer is good. But we say . . . that it is the beginning of the

Reprinted by permission of Kirk Anderson.

The petitioners in Engel v. Vitale *were careful to explain that they were not opposed to religion itself, only to the teaching of it in government-run public schools.*

end of religious freedom when religious activity such as this [prayer] is incorporated into the public school system of the United States. . . . Where the avowed purpose of the state is to promote religion, one religion, all religions—then this activity is barred by the First Amendment.[21]

The Respondents Present Their Arguments

After speaking and answering questions for almost an hour, Butler finished his presentation and sat down. It was now the respondents' turn to present arguments, and Bertram B. Daiker, representing the school board, strode confidently to the lectern. Like Butler, his first argument invoked the First Amendment; however, Daiker emphasized the issue of freedom of expression. The prayer did not constitute a form of religious instruction, as the petitioners seemed to suggest, he insisted, but instead a form of religious expression. He admitted that the content of the prayer was religious, but reciting it in the classroom constituted only a voluntary exercise of the children's faith. And most importantly, that kind of personal expression was guaranteed by the First Amendment. The children said the same prayer each day without any commentary by the teacher or anyone else, Daiker pointed out, so it could not be construed as a form of instruction.

Next, Daiker made the same point that some of the judges in the lower courts had—namely that prayer was an integral part of America's spiritual heritage. "An avowal of faith in a Supreme Being is fully in accord with our traditions,"[22] he said. As examples, he cited the constitutions of forty-nine states, each of which refers to God; the Declaration of Independence, which also mentions "the Creator"; American coins, which bear the words *In God We Trust;* and other similar documents and institutions, such as the Gettysburg Address, the National Anthem, and the presidential oath of office.

The third argument Daiker presented was that the prayer in question was not compulsory, as the petitioners claimed. "There is no direct compulsion by the school authorities compelling the child

The respondents in Engel v. Vitale *argued that the prayer was part of America's heritage and that faith in a Supreme Being was evident in many historical documents, including the Gettysburg Address written by Abraham Lincoln.*

to pray,"[23] he said. Any student who desired to be excused from the exercise could do so after submitting a written request by a parent.

Furthermore, Daiker argued, the prayer was very short, taking only about thirty seconds to recite. It was also harmless, for there was no evidence whatsoever that any one of the thousands of children who had recited it since 1958 had been harmed in any way. Therefore, the issue of its use in the classroom was too trivial to waste the time of the U.S. Supreme Court, whose time should be reserved for weightier matters.

Another point Daiker made was that the regents' prayer did not favor one religious group over another. The words *Almighty God* and various other phrases in the prayer were universally recognized by most faiths, he insisted. And even if there did exist a small handful of parents and students who did not recognize these phrases and were offended by them, they had the right, as stated earlier, to refrain from saying them. "For these reasons," Daiker said,

> voluntary expressions of belief in God should not be abolished because they are allegedly in conflict with the beliefs of some. . . . Those who object because of an alleged conflict with their belief should be permitted to refrain from participating . . . but there should not be an abolition of such voluntary recital.[24]

Finally, Daiker brought up the issue of morality. The Board of Regents had instituted the prayer partly to provide moral training for the students, he pointed out. They had done so because they were concerned about a reported rise in juvenile delinquency in the country and hoped that having the students say a short prayer every day would keep them from becoming delinquents later. According to this argument, removing prayer from the classroom might well damage the moral sense of the students and worsen, rather than improve, the behavior of American children.

Porter R. Chandler, who represented the sixteen New Hyde Park parents who wanted the prayer to continue, spoke next. His main argument, which covered some ground that Daiker's arguments had not, maintained that the petitioners were damaging the rights of other Americans who did not agree with them. Those who did not like the prayer, Chandler said, had the right to be excused but *not* the right to impose their views on everyone else by having the prayer abolished. In essence, he said, the petitioners were preying on others' rights to give voice, through prayer, to their cherished traditions of faith:

> They [the petitioners] deny to any public school the right to suggest to any child that God is our Creator and the Author of our liberties or to encourage any public expression of gratitude to Him for those liberties, regardless of the wishes of the child or his parents and regardless of the historical and constitutional tradition of this nation.[25]

Chandler also noted that the Supreme Court had earlier upheld the rights of the Jehovah's Witnesses (a fundamentalist Christian sect) to have their children excused from the flag salute. But the Jehovah's Witnesses had not insisted on banning the flag salute altogether from the classroom, which would clearly have denied the rights of those who wanted to continue reciting the salute.

The Justices Raise the Issues of Compulsion and Indoctrination

As they had done during Butler's argument, the justices interrupted the respondents' lawyers with various queries. One of the most pointed of the exchanges was between Daiker and Justice Felix Frankfurter and Chief Justice Earl Warren, on the issues of tradition and compulsion. "You say it isn't teaching religion to take for granted that [set of cherished traditions] which [underlie] all our national life?"[26] Frankfurter asked.

"That's right," Daiker answered. "It [the recital of the prayer] is simply an avowal of everything we have learned since we were children." As another example of an accepted tradition involving the recognition of God, Daiker noted that the Supreme Court's crier begins each session by saying, "God save the United States and this Honorable Court."[27]

But Earl Warren questioned this comparison. "I wonder whether it would make a difference if we were to require every litigant and lawyer who comes in here to say the same prayer your school district requires."[28]

Daiker responded that such a requirement might raise the question of compulsion. Seeing that Warren was drawing a comparison between requiring lawyers to say a prayer and requiring children in school to do so, Daiker readily conceded that if the regents' prayer were compulsory, it would be unconstitutional. In such a scenario, he said, the state would be taking advantage of the fact that schoolchildren are a captive audience.

"So the case gets down to the question of whether the circumstances of the prayer's recital differentiates this [requirement] from frank compulsion,"[29] Frankfurter said. He then recalled the case of *Vidal v. Girard's Executors*, in which Stephen Girard had stipulated in his will that no priests or other religious leaders should ever set foot in a school built with his money. One of the main issues in that case, Frankfurter maintained, was whether allowing religious leaders to teach children posed a danger of indoctrinating the students with religious beliefs. He suggested that young children were especially susceptible to religious indoctrination, and he wondered whether such indoctrination could be interpreted as a form of compulsion.

Justice Felix Frankfurter was concerned about the susceptibility of young children to religious indoctrination.

A New York Judge Foreshadows the Supreme Court

One dissenter on the New York Court of Appeals, when that panel rejected the petition brought by Steven Engel and the other New Hyde Park parents, used reasoning remarkably similar to that used by the majority on the Supreme Court a year later. As quoted in Sam Duker's *The Public Schools and Religion*, this dissenting opinion reads, in part,

> The Sponsors of the Regent's prayer claim that it is non-sectarian in nature, a simple statement acknowledging the existence of and our dependence upon a Supreme Being; that such reference is of much the same character as the reference to God in various holiday programs (i.e., Christmas, Easter, Thanksgiving Day), in various official oaths, in invocations and benedictions said at most public gatherings, at meetings of some official bodies, as well as in the inscription of the motto "In God We Trust" on coins, stamps, and bank notes. Although these references may well be regarded as a permissible illustration that we are a religious people . . . it does not follow that the Regent's prayer is beyond the reach of the First Amendment. Such an approach belies the avowed purpose of the Regents, which, as we have pointed out, was to commence "teaching our children [about respect for God]." In our view, this conflicts with the establishment clause [of the First Amendment].

Daiker emphatically denied that students in the New Hyde Park schools were being subjected to any sectarian or other kind of religious indoctrination. Furthermore, he declared, in trying to safeguard against indoctrination that did not in fact exist, the petitioners were trying to remove any recognition of God from the public schools, which was potentially more damaging to the students than any form of religious training. "They attack not only the Regents' prayer," he said, "but any form of prayer whatsoever."[30]

The question-and-answer session between the justices and attorneys lasted for almost three hours. When it was over, each side was confident that it had made a strong case. But the lawyers had learned from experience that it would be unwise to be overconfident before hearing the final decision, and they advised their respective clients to this effect. In the weeks that followed, they, along with millions of other interested people around the nation, waited anxiously to see whether school prayer would be upheld or abolished.

Chapter 4

The High Court Decides in Favor of the Petitioners

O N JUNE 25, 1962, two months after hearing the case, the Supreme Court issued its ruling in *Engel v. Vitale*. The decision was in favor of the petitioners, the New Hyde Park parents who had argued that the Board of Regents' prayer was unconstitutional. The vote was six to one, with Justices Earl Warren, Hugo Black, William O. Douglas, Tom C. Clark, William C. Brennan Jr., and John M. Harlan voting to ban the prayer, and Potter Stewart voting to retain the prayer. Two justices had abstained from the vote—Byron R. White and Felix Frankfurter—both citing personal reasons. Justice Black wrote the majority opinion (a statement that explains why the majority of the judges have voted a certain way); Justice Douglas composed a concurring opinion (to explain his own reasons for voting with the majority); and Justice Stewart wrote the dissenting opinion.

A Contradiction of the Establishment Clause

The first point made by Justice Black in the majority opinion was that the regents' prayer was unconstitutional because it was an example of the government's sponsoring of a specific religious practice. This, he said, contradicted the establishment clause of the First Amendment, which forbids the government from officially supporting a particular religion or religion in general. "We think that by using the public school system to encourage recitation of the Regent's prayer," he began,

the State of New York has adopted a practice wholly inconsistent with the establishment clause. There can be no
doubt, of course, that New York's program of daily classroom
invocation of God's blessings as prescribed in the Regent's
prayer is a religious activity. It is a solemn avowal of divine
faith and supplication for the blessings of the Almighty. . . .
The petitioners contend among other things that the state
laws requiring or permitting the use of the Regents' prayer
must be struck down as a violation of the establishment
clause. . . . We agree with that contention since we think that
the constitutional prohibition against laws respecting an
establishment of religion must at least mean that in this
country it is no part of the business of government to com-
pose official prayers for any group of the American people to
recite as part of a religious program carried on by the government.[31]

To support this view, Black then cited historical evidence showing
that America's founders had good reason to ensure the separation of
church and state, including government-composed and government-
sponsored prayers. "It is a matter of history," he wrote,

that this very practice of
establishing governmen-
tally composed prayers
for religious services was
one of the reasons which
caused many of our early
colonists to leave England
and seek religious free-
dom in America. The
Book of Common Prayer,
which was created under
[English] governmental

*Justice Hugo Black voted that the
Board of Regents' prayer was
unconstitutional.*

direction . . . set out in minute detail the accepted form and content of prayer and other religious ceremonies to be used in the established, tax-supported Church of England. The controversies over the Book and what should be its content repeatedly threatened to disrupt the peace of that country. . . . [Because of such incidents]

JUSTICE HUGO BLACK

Hugo Lafayette Black was born in the hill country of Alabama in 1886, where his father was a businessman of Scottish-Irish descent. Raised in an era of strict segregation, Black was at one time a member of the Ku Klux Klan (KKK). In 1927 Black was elected to the U.S. Senate as a Democrat and was a supporter of President Franklin D. Roosevelt's New Deal policies. Eventually, in 1937, Black became Roosevelt's first appointment to the Supreme Court. Shortly after his swearing-in, but prior to taking his seat on the bench, newspapers reported Black's involvement with the KKK. Black explained that he had indeed joined as a young man, but that he had later resigned from the organization and come to reject its racist views. Despite protesters who filed a petition to deny Black his seat on the Supreme Court, he remained a justice until 1971, when he retired following a stroke. He was often labeled an activist because of his willingness to review legislation that arguably violated constitutional provisions.

A Ku Klux Klan initiation ceremony, circa 1920.

by the time of the adoption of the [U.S.] Constitution, our history shows that there was a widespread awareness among many Americans of the dangers of a union of Church and State. . . . The Constitution was intended to avert a part of this danger by leaving the government of this country in the hands of the people rather than in the hands of any monarch. But this safeguard was not enough. Our founders were no more willing to let the content of

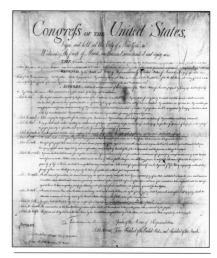

The Supreme Court decided the Regents' prayer was unconstitutional because it contradicted the establishment clause of the Constitution's First Amendment.

their prayers and their privilege of praying whenever they pleased be influenced by the ballot box than they were to let these vital matters of personal conscience depend upon the succession of monarchs. . . . The First Amendment was added to the Constitution to stand as a guarantee that neither the power nor the prestige of the Federal Government would be used to control, support, or influence the kinds of prayer the American people can say.[32]

Several of the Respondents' Arguments Are Rejected

Black's majority opinion also specifically addressed and rejected several of the arguments made by the respondents in their support of the prayer. Among these were the arguments that the prayer was both nondenominational and short and was therefore insignificant and an issue unworthy of the Court's attention. Black admitted that the prayer was indeed "relatively insignificant when compared to the governmental encroachments upon religion which were commonplace two hundred years ago."[33] However, he continued, even a brief and general prayer might constitute a dangerous precedent

BLACK ON THE GENIUS OF THE FIRST AMENDMENT

The justices filed into the Supreme Court to their respective chairs on the bench on Tuesday, June 26, 1962, and sat down to read their decision on *Engel v. Vitale*. Justice Hugo Black took the honors of reading the majority opinion, then sat back in his chair to comment on the case. Among his spontaneous comments were these, which were later reported in the *New York Times* and other newspapers: "The prayer of each man from his soul must be his and his alone. That is the genius of the First Amendment. . . . If there is any one thing clear in the First Amendment it is that the right of the people to pray in their own way is not to be controlled by the election returns."

of governmental establishment of religion; as evidence he cited James Madison, author of the First Amendment:

[It] is proper to take alarm at the first [instance of] experiment[ation] on [i.e., tampering with] our liberties. . . . Who does not see that the same authority which can establish Christianity, in exclusion of all other religions, may establish with the same ease any particular sect of Christians, in exclusion of all other sects? That the same authority which can force a citizen to contribute three pence only of his property for the support of any one establishment, may force him to conform to any other establishment in all cases whatsoever?[34]

Next, Justice Black dealt with the respondents' argument that the prayer was strictly voluntary because students had the option of not taking part. This view, he said, overlooked the fact that a law or policy sponsored by the government did not have to specify compulsory behavior directly for compulsion to be present. Instead, the very fact of the government's financial sponsorship and support of a particular belief creates indirect pressure for everyone, including those opposed to the belief, to conform to it. "When the power, prestige, and financial support of the government is placed behind a particular religious belief," he wrote, "the indirect coercive pressure upon religious minorities to conform to the prevailing officially approved religion is plain."[35]

In addition, Black responded to Attorney Daiker's argument that the petitioners were in effect coming out not only against the Regents' prayer but also against prayer in general and that banning prayer would be hostile to both prayer and religion. "Nothing, of course, could be further from the truth," said Black. America's founders were well aware that the First Amendment, which put an end to government control of religion and prayer, was not written to destroy either of these cherished institutions. After all, these were all highly religious men who staunchly supported the idea and practice of prayer. Rather, Black explained, they wrote the First Amendment

to quiet well-justified fears which nearly all of them felt arising out of an awareness that governments of the past had shackled men's tongues to make them speak only the religious thoughts that government wanted them to speak and to pray only to the God that government wanted them to pray to. It is neither sacrilegious nor anti-religious to say that each separate government in this country [whether federal, state, or local] should stay out of the business of writing or sanctioning official prayers and leave that purely religious function to the people themselves and to those the people choose to look to for religious guidance.[36]

James Madison, fourth president of the United States and the author of the First Amendment.

Justice Douglas Takes Aim at Government-Financed Religion

In his concurring opinion, Justice Douglas agreed with the majority opinion and went even further. His main contention was that, according to the intent of the Constitution, the government should not and could not be involved in the financing of a religious activity. "The question presented by this case," he stated, "is therefore an extremely narrow one. It is whether New York oversteps the bounds [of its constitutional authority] when it finances a religious exercise."[37]

Douglas elaborated on this statement. On the face of it, he said, what New York did by including prayer in its opening classroom exercises was no different than what the crier for the Supreme Court did when he said "God save the United States and this Honorable Court" at the beginning of a court session. In both cases, people were free either to join or not to join in the observance. The difference was that the chaplains saying the prayer in the courtroom were "guests" of the Court and unpaid volunteers; in contrast, the teachers administering and saying the prayer in New York's schools were on the public payroll and were therefore involved in governmental sponsorship of religion. This clearly violated the language of the First Amendment. It did not matter that the prayer was short and that its administration and recital took very little of the teachers' time. "For me the principle is the same," Douglas wrote,

no matter how briefly the prayer is said, for in each of the instances given, the person praying is a public official on the public payroll, performing a religious exercise in a governmental institution. . . . I cannot say that to authorize this prayer is to establish a religion in the strictly historical meaning of those words. . . . Yet

Justice William Douglas believed the government should not finance any religious activity.

once government finances a religious exercise, it inserts a divisive influence into our communities.[38]

Justice Douglas also suggested that the prayer in question was only one of many instances of government-financed religious activity that could be construed as unconstitutional. In fact, he said, "our system at the federal and state levels is presently honeycombed with such financing."[39] For examples, Douglas quoted from noted legal historian David Fellman's *The Limits of Freedom:*

> There are many "aids" to religion in this country at all levels of government. To mention but a few at the federal level . . . there is compulsory chapel at the service academies, and religious services are held in federal hospitals and prisons. The president issues religious proclamations. The Bible is used for the administration of oaths. . . . Veterans receiving money under the "G.I." Bill of 1944 [which helps finance their higher education] could attend denominational [i.e., religious] schools to which payments were made directly by the government. . . . The slogan "In God We Trust" is issued [on currency] by the Treasury Department, and Congress recently added God to the pledge of allegiance. . . . [In addition] religious organizations are exempt from federal income tax and are granted postal privileges.[40]

By citing these examples, Douglas implied that the *Engel v. Vitale* case and the Supreme Court's decision in favor of the petitioners had opened wide the possibility of future legal challenges to other government-financed religious activities that millions of people took for granted.

The Lone Dissenter Speaks

Justice Stewart began his dissenting opinion with a firm affirmation of his disagreement with the majority and concurring opinions. "The Court," he wrote, "today decides that in permitting this brief, non-denominational prayer the school board has violated the Constitution of the United States. I think this decision is wrong."[41] Stewart's main point of disagreement related to the issue of the First Amendment.

To say that the recital of the regents' prayer violated that statute, he maintained, would necessitate the establishment of an official religion, as stated in the so-called establishment clause. However, in his view the Board of Regents had done no such thing when they instituted the prayer. "With all respect," Stewart said,

> I think the Court has misapplied a great constitutional principle. I cannot see how an "official religion" is established by letting those who want to say a prayer say it. On the contrary, I think to deny the wish of these school children to join in reciting this prayer is to deny them the opportunity of sharing in the spiritual heritage of our nation.[42]

Justice Potter Stewart, the only dissenter in the Engel v. Vitale *case.*

Stewart went on to reject the majority opinion's citing of the historical case of the Book of Common Prayer. In England, he pointed out, there was an officially established church, but the United States had no established church. Thus, there was no valid comparison between the two situations. Since the Constitution forbade the establishment of a state church, and because the early colonies disestablished colonial churches so that they could not become state churches, the U.S. government could never recognize and sponsor one religious denomination over all others. "We deal here not with the establishment of a state church," he wrote, "but with whether school children who want to begin their day by joining in prayer must be prohibited from doing so."[43]

Next, Stewart recalled some of the many religious manifestations that Douglas, in his concurring opinion, had claimed "honeycombed" the American governmental system. Among these were the National Anthem, the inscription "In God We Trust" on coins, the phrase *under God* in the pledge of allegiance, the opening of congressional sessions with a prayer, and so forth. But unlike Douglas, who questioned the constitutionality of these examples, Stewart held that they were acceptable, cherished traditions. Moreover, he insisted, these religious manifestations were no different in character and intent than the Regents' prayer. To strengthen this point, Stewart provided an impressive list of U.S. presidents who had, in their speeches, publicly asked for God's aid and protection, including George Washington, John Adams, Thomas Jefferson, Abraham Lincoln, Grover Cleveland, Woodrow Wilson, Franklin D. Roosevelt, Dwight D. Eisenhower, and John F. Kennedy. "I do not believe that this Court," Stewart said, "or the Congress, or the president has by the actions and practices I have mentioned established an 'official religion' in violation of the Constitution. And I do not believe the State of New York has done so in this case."[44]

School Prayer Officially Banned

Despite Potter's eloquent, solitary protest, that day the majority of his colleagues decided the course the country would take in the matter

Justice Stewart: Profile of a "Swing Man"

The lone voice of dissent standing against the majority opinion in the *Engel v. Vitale* case, Justice Potter Stewart, was often called a "swing man" for his tendency to cast the decisive vote in an otherwise evenly divided court. Stewart was born in 1915 in Jackson, Michigan, although his family later moved to Cincinnati, Ohio. Stewart's father later became the Republican mayor of Cincinnati, so the boy grew up with an appreciation of politics. After graduating from Yale Law School in 1941, Stewart served with the U.S. Naval Reserve during World War II, then practiced law for several years. In 1954 he became a judge of the U.S. Court of Appeals, Sixth Circuit, and in 1958 President Dwight D. Eisenhower appointed him to the Supreme Court, on which he served until retiring in 1981.

of school prayer. As Justice Black officially stated in the conclusion of the majority opinion, "The judgment of the Court of Appeals of New York is reversed and the case remanded [sent back] for further proceedings not inconsistent with this opinion."[45] In other words, the Supreme Court had overturned the decisions made earlier by the lower courts, and it was now unlawful for public schools in the United States to sponsor, administer, or otherwise introduce or take part in prayers.

George Washington was one of many U.S. presidents who publicly asked for God's aid and protection.

The petitioners were satisfied and relieved that their position had prevailed, of course. Still, they realized that the Court's decision was unprecedented and potentially controversial and divisive. They were fully aware that they remained in the minority and expected that many Americans would be unhappy with the High Court's decision. But as they exited the building that day, they were unprepared for the veritable avalanche of angry reactions that would soon sweep the nation and dominate reports in the news media.

Chapter 5

The Court's Decision Stirs Up Controversy

WITHIN THE TWENTY-FOUR hours following the Supreme Court's decision in *Engel v. Vitale*, people all over the country began to react. Among the more prominent of those expressing opinions were two former presidents—Herbert Hoover and Dwight D. Eisenhower. Hoover, who had served as president from 1929 to 1933, called the decision a "disintegration of a sacred American heritage."[46] Eisenhower, who had served from 1953 to 1961, was also critical, pointing out that school prayer was a long-accepted tradition on a par with references to God appearing in the Declaration of Independence and other cherished national documents.

Meanwhile, ten U.S. congressmen introduced bitter attacks on the Supreme Court into the *Congressional Record*, and newspaper editorials across the country denounced the ruling. At the same time, hundreds of religious spokesmen voiced their objections.

Former president Herbert Hoover, one of many disappointed in the Engel v. Vitale *ruling.*

61

ONE OF THE FEW MODERATE REACTIONS
TO THE *ENGEL* RULING

Most of the immediate public reactions to the Supreme Court's ruling in *Engel v. Vitale* were either strongly in favor of or strongly against the decision. A few, however, like this tract from the July 23, 1962, edition of the publication *Christianity and Crisis*, attempted to take a more moderate, middle-of-the-road approach.

> The religious heritage of the nation does not depend on the presence of this prayer in the opening exercises of the New York schoolroom. Yet the Court decision holding the prayer to be in violation of the First Amendment to the constitution has created a furor of positive and negative responses. This reaction reveals that symbols, rather than facts, were involved as they so frequently are in both religious and political controversies. The Regent's prayer was a symbol of the religious life and tradition of the nation. The Court decision symbolizes to some religious people the perils of secularization of our culture. Religious opinion on the matter was sharply divided. The most devastating criticism came from [New York's] Cardinal [Francis J.] Spellman, though his concern seemed in contradiction to the Roman Catholic criticism of the public schools as "godless." The religious champions of the separation of church and state, chiefly the Baptists, were not unanimous in their approval. . . . The question that must be raised in the aftermath of the [Court's] decision is whether it will not work so consistently in the direction of a secularization of the school system as to amount to the suppression of religion and to give the impression that government must be anti-religion. This impression is certainly not consonant with the mood of either the Founding Fathers or our long tradition of separation of church and state, which is based on neutrality and not animosity.

Contributing to this heavily negative reaction was the fact that much of the mass media reporting was factually sketchy and often inaccurate, which resulted in confusion over the Court's actual ruling.

Reactions by ordinary citizens were also largely negative, especially when people realized that the *Engel v. Vitale* case was not simply about New York State policy. Realizing that the High Court's ban on prayer in the schools would be applied in all states, many people were shocked and upset. They not only strongly disagreed with the ruling but also worried about the possibility of more court "attacks" on religion. One fear commonly expressed was that the government might proceed to ban other religious traditions in public life, such as the appearance of "In God We Trust" on coins and the use of the Bible in swearing-in ceremonies for public officials. Justice Black had carefully drafted the majority opinion in such a way as to dispel such fears, but most Americans did not actually read the text of that opinion. Over the next month, the High Court received approximately five thousand letters, most of them critical of the ruling.

Not all public reaction to the ruling on school prayer was negative, however. President John F. Kennedy, a devout Catholic, was conciliatory, saying that the Supreme Court was well within its rights to rule the way it did. "I would think it would be a welcome reminder to every American family," he added, "that we can pray a good deal more at home and attend our churches with a good deal more fidelity."[47] In addition, a significant minority of Americans expressed positive feelings about the ruling. To them, the Supreme Court's decision meant that their religious freedoms were protected from government influence.

Congressional Reactions

The intensity of public reaction to the Court's ruling was slow to die down. Among the most audible and widely reported attacks occurred in the U.S. Congress. First, some congressmen made disparaging remarks, both public and private, that soon were reported by the media. One member of Congress, Frank J. Becker, a Republican from New York, called the ruling the most tragic ever made in the country's history. Others took the opportunity to express their displeasure over other Supreme Court rulings. Representative George Andrews, an Alabama Democrat, remarked that first blacks were being admitted to formerly all-white schools and that now religion had been banned from these same schools, referring to earlier Supreme Court rulings ordering an end to racial segregation in schools. Still other congressmen attempted to play to the public's Cold War–era fears of Communist Russia. John J. Rooney, a New York Democrat, warned that the *Engel v. Vitale* ruling could put U.S. schools on the same basis as Russian schools, in which even the mention of God was not permitted.

Many in Congress used the Engel v. Vitale *decision to criticize other rulings such as the decision allowing blacks to attend all-white schools.*

A number of congressmen also went beyond mere rhetoric and introduced resolutions in support of school prayer. Though these statements had no legal force, they were an official way to show congressional displeasure with the Supreme Court's decision. In the two years following the *Engel v. Vitale* ruling, some 115 members of the House of Representatives introduced 151 such resolutions; the Senate drafted another eleven.

A few congressman decided to go even further and attempt to undo the Supreme Court's decision by proposing a constitutional amendment specifically allowing prayer in public schools. Congressman Becker, a devout Catholic and strong supporter of public schools, devoted himself to drafting and passing such an amendment; he managed to get the House Judiciary Committee to hold hearings on the proposed amendment in April 1964. The hearings lasted for eighteen days and included the testimony of religious leaders, lawyers, and politicians. Of the thirteen thousand letters the committee received during the hearings, a majority were in favor of a constitutional amendment, so Becker was hopeful that the initiative would succeed.

The House failed to approve the school-prayer amendment, however. This was partly because the influential chairman of the committee, New York congressman Emmanuel Celler, was opposed to prayer in the schools, believing that it violated the First Amendment. Even more damaging to the effort to pass the amendment was the testimony of over 220 widely respected professors of constitutional law. They almost unanimously opposed such an amendment, saying that America's founders had crafted the Bill of Rights to provide basic rights regardless of the will of the majority on any given issue. Leo Pfeffer, an authority on the First Amendment, who had assisted William J. Butler in preparing the petitioners' brief for *Engel v. Vitale*, summed up this view when he said, "If you open the door for constitutional amendments because a particular decision at a particular time is unpopular, the entire purpose of the Bill of Rights to ride out periods of passion will have been destroyed."[48]

Religious Reactions

Religious reactions to the *Engel v. Vitale* ruling varied widely. Some noted religious leaders were clearly upset by and opposed to the

New York congressman and chairman of the House Judiciary Committee, Emmanuel Celler, opposed prayer in schools.

ruling, seeing it as a direct attack on religious tradition and a potential threat to the moral upbringing of American children. Catholic leaders appeared to be particularly offended and outraged. New York's cardinal Francis J. Spellman, for example, said, "The decision strikes at the very heart of the godly tradition in which America's children have for so long been raised."[49] Spellman's colleague, Cardinal James F. McIntyre of Los Angeles, concurred, saying, "The decision is positively shocking and scandalizing to one of American blood and principles. It is not only a decision according to law, but a decision of license."[50] This license of the Court, he went on to say, denied children the right to speak to their Creator. McIntyre also suggested that the decision was the kind one might expect from leaders in the Soviet Union. Another Catholic leader, Cardinal Cushing of Boston, also drew comparisons with the Soviets and warned that they would likely use the Supreme Court's ruling to create anti-American propaganda.

New York's Cardinal Francis J. Spellman (standing, left) condemned the Engel v. Vitale *ruling.*

Spokesmen for many Protestant denominations also condemned the ruling. The National Association of Evangelicals termed the ruling regrettable, and popular evangelist Billy Graham said it seemed to be part of a trend in which more and more people were distancing themselves from religion and morality. The Reverend Arthur L. Kinsolving, president of the Protestant Council of the City of New York and pastor of St. James Protestant Episcopal Church, concurred with this assessment; he expressed the hope that the country's moral decay could be reversed. "Ultimately," he remarked, "we will have to review the [Supreme Court's] decision and find some way back to the religious foundations of this country."[51] Still another Protestant leader, James A. Pike, bishop of the Episcopal Diocese of California, stated that he thought the decision misconstrued the intent of America's founders in authoring the First Amendment. In Pike's view, in passing that amendment, Madison, Jefferson, and the others clearly did not intend to inhibit the free exercise of religious traditions.

In stark contrast, however, a number of religious leaders and organizations expressed support for the *Engel v. Vitale* ruling. They typically said it preserved religious freedom and diversity by keeping one faith or sect from promoting its views in the public schools and that it kept American democracy strong and independent of coercion by ensuring continued separation of church and state. Spokesmen for the Anti-Defamation League of B'nai B'rith, for example, called the decision "a splendid affirmation of a basic American principle . . . [that] adds another safeguard for freedom of religion in the United States."[52] A. M. Sonnabend, president of the American Jewish Committee, said that the ruling affirmed that prayer in America's democratic society was a matter for the home, synagogue, and church, and not for state institutions. Dean Kelly, a prominent director of the National Council of Churches, agreed. "It [the ruling] protects the religious rights of minorities," he said, "and guards against the development of 'public school religion,' which is neither Christianity nor Judaism, but something less than either [of these great faiths]."[53] Dana McLean, president of the Unitarian Universalist Association, also voiced his strong support of the ruling.

Varying Degrees of Compliance

Just as important as the political and religious reactions to the *Engel v. Vitale* ruling was the reaction of local school boards around the country. They were, after all, the parties most immediately affected by the decision of the High Court. A good many school boards complied with the ruling immediately, one of them being the New York State Board of Regents, whose prayer had initiated the controversy in the first place. The board assured reporters that the state's schools would comply and remove the prayer from classrooms. At the same time, the board vigorously defended itself and its prior actions and continued to maintain that school prayer was not a bad thing. William Vitale, who had headed the New Hyde Park school board when the case began, reiterated that

> at no time did we ever insist that a child should say it [the prayer]. We set up mechanics [here meaning accommodation for those who did not wish to participate] so that no one would be compelled to say it and we felt sincerely we were not infringing on anyone's constitutional rights.[54]

It is difficult to tell exactly how many school systems nationwide complied with the Supreme Court ruling and eliminated school prayer. A privately conducted 1965 survey of school officials was designed to measure compliance, but the officials were not obligated to respond to the survey, and some did not; also, some claimed that they did not have accurate figures about compliance in all of the schools in their systems. The results of the survey nonetheless indicated that about 19 percent of the public schools sampled were still conducting some kind of prayer recital or similar devotional exercise as of 1965. These exercises included such long-standing traditions as members of a school's football team praying before games, devotionals during morning broadcasts over the school's public-address system, individual teachers expressing their religious beliefs in the classroom, and having a moment of silent prayer before class commenced.

The degree of compliance also varied from region to region. In the South, for instance, about 52 percent of schools still conducted some kind of prayer three years after the *Engel v. Vitale* ruling; in

It has been difficult to determine if schools are complying with the Supreme Court's decision in the Engel v. Vitale *case.*

the West, where school prayer had been less prevalent to begin with, fewer than 3 percent of schools were still conducting prayers and other devotionals in 1965.

This and other surveys found that, in addition, a good many school systems attempted to get around the High Court's ruling by creating prayers that left out the terms *God* and *Jesus Christ*. In Illinois in 1965, for example, some schools began using a popular prayer, the last line of which originally read, "We thank you, God, for everything." School officials removed the word God, so that the line read: "We thank you for everything." But a number of parents found this unacceptable and some of them sued. An Illinois court of appeals ruled that the verse was a prayer, with or without the term *God*, and was therefore unconstitutional.

The *Engel* Case Serves as a Precedent

The judges in the Illinois case and others hearing similar cases in other states relied heavily on the Supreme Court's reasoning and opinions in the *Engel v. Vitale* case. In fact, other cases involving religious exercises in public schools came before the Supreme

The Schempp family won their case in the Supreme Court. The justices based their decision on the precedent set by Engel v. Vitale.

Court in the same period and the High Court relied on its own decision in *Engel v. Vitale.* The most famous of these cases was *Abington School District v. Schempp,* in which the Court issued its ruling on June 17, 1963.

The *Schempp* case grew out of a dispute about Bible readings in Pennsylvania classrooms in the early 1960s. A state law called for the reading of ten or more verses from the Bible during morning exercises; as in the *Engel* case, students who did not want to participate could present a letter of excuse from their parents. This arrangement was not satisfactory, however, to Edward Schempp and his wife, Sidney, whose three children attended school in Germantown, just outside of Philadelphia. The Schempps felt that

THE *SCHEMPP* RULING DRAWS ON THE *ENGEL* CASE

In *Abington School District v. Schempp*, the Supreme Court sided with the petitioner and ruled that Bible readings in a public-school classroom were unconstitutional. In this excerpt from his opinion, as quoted in Sam Duker's *The Public Schools and Religion*, Justice Tom C. Clark's reliance on the precedent of *Engel v. Vitale* is clear.

It is true that religion has been closely identified with our history and government. As we said in *Engel v. Vitale* . . . "The history of man is inseparable from the history of religion." . . . The fact that the founding fathers believed devotedly that there was a God and that the unalienable rights of man were rooted in Him is clearly evidenced in their writings, from the Mayflower Compact to the Constitution itself. This background is evidenced today in our public life through the continuance of our oaths of office. . . . Likewise, each House of Congress provides through its Chaplain an opening prayer. . . . Indeed, only last year an official survey of the country indicated that 64 percent of our people have church membership . . . while less than 3 percent profess no religion whatever. . . . It can truly be said, therefore, that today, as in the beginning, our national life reflects a [highly] religious people. . . . This is not to say, however, that religion has been so identified with our history and our government that religious freedom is not likewise so strongly imbedded in our public and private life. . . . This court had decisively settled that the First Amendment's mandate that "Congress shall make no law respecting an establishment of religion or prohibiting the free exercise thereof" has been made wholly applicable to the states by the Fourteenth Amendment. . . . [At the same time] this court had rejected unequivocally the contention that the establishment clause forbids only governmental preference of one religion over another. . . . We agree with the trial court's finding as to the religious character of the [religious] exercises [in question]. Given that finding, the exercises and the law requiring them are in violation of the establishment clause.

References to God exist in many early writings, including the Mayflower Compact.

forcing their children to listen to Bible readings was against their Unitarian beliefs. They also said that excusing their children from these devotional exercises was potentially damaging because it would likely result in the children being labeled oddballs, outcasts, or, even worse in their eyes, atheists.

The Schempps took the school district to court and won. But the school district decided to appeal and the case made it to the Supreme Court, which also ruled in favor of the Schempps. This time Justice Tom C. Clark wrote the majority opinion. Just as Justice Hugo Black had done in his opinion in the *Engel* case, Clark acknowledged that Americans were traditionally a religious people who presupposed the existence of a supreme being. But he pointed out that the First Amendment's establishment clause mandates the separation of church and state. In a comprehensive concurring opinion, Justice William C. Brennan Jr. echoed Black's argument in *Engel*—that recital of the Regents' prayer had been accompanied by an atmosphere of peer pressure to participate. Brennan wrote that the Pennsylvania Bible readings put students in a "cruel dilemma" because of their fear of ridicule. "Even devout children," he suggested, "may well avoid claiming their right [to be excused from the readings] and simply continue to participate in exercises distasteful to them because of an understandable reluctance to be stigmatized as atheists or nonconformists simply on the basis of their request."[55]

Brennan's opinion made several references to the *Engel* case as a precedent. Meanwhile, Justice Potter Stewart delivered the lone dissenting opinion, just as he had done in *Engel v. Vitale;* as in that case, he took exception with the majority's interpretation of the First Amendment's establishment clause.

Clearly, the Supreme Court's support of the petitioners in the 1962 *Engel* case had opened the door to other challenges to religious practices in American public schools. What no one in the early 1960s could have known for certain was that such challenges would continue to come before the High Court for the remainder of the twentieth century. Moreover, in some of these new cases, the issue of school prayer would resurface repeatedly, showing that the Supreme Court's 1962 ruling was far from the last word on the matter.

Chapter 6

The War over Prayer in the Schools Continues

COURT CASES STEMMING FROM disputes over religious activities, including prayer, in schools continued in the 1970s, 1980s, and 1990s. And the *Engel v. Vitale* ruling continued to be an important precedent used by judges ruling in such cases. Some of these disputes were the result of open noncompliance with the *Engel* ruling. Those who chose not to comply typically felt that the government had shown disrespect for, or even animosity toward, religion. Other cases sought to test further the limits of separation of church and state in the wake of the *Engel* and *Schempp* cases. And still others resulted from public confusion over what the *Engel* and *Schempp* rulings actually meant. Most commonly, interpretation of these rulings was left up to the individual school districts. Some districts interpreted the rulings to mean that school prayers and Bible readings were constitutional so long as students were not compelled to participate or so long as the students themselves initiated the activity.

The *Jaffree* Case Revives the Controversy

One of the most important and controversial cases dealing with school prayer in recent years was the 1985 *Wallace v. Jaffree* case. By the 1980s twenty-five states had passed laws that permitted or provided for moments of silence in public-school classrooms, brief interludes for either personal reflection or voluntary personal prayer. To many school officials, these moments of silence seemed to be a legitimate way of including prayer in the classroom without

73

Ishmael Jaffree, seen here in front of the Supreme Court, successfully challenged the moment of silence in the Mobile, Alabama public school system.

openly defying the *Engel* ruling, which dealt with the more overt recital of prayers.

But this moment of silence was challenged in 1985 in Mobile, Alabama. Ishmael Jaffree, the father of three students in the Mobile school system, felt that the moment of silence was a veiled religious practice, and he sued the local school board, hoping to get the exercise removed from the classroom. A federal court of appeals found in Jaffree's favor and struck down the Alabama law that permitted such interludes. The school board appealed to the Supreme Court, which upheld the ruling of the lower court. Alabama's law authorizing a period of silence for meditation or prayer, the Court ruled, violated the First Amendment.

The court was particularly worried about the underlying purpose of the Alabama law. In his majority opinion, Justice John P. Stevens wrote,

> The prime sponsor of the bill . . . explained that the bill was an "effort to return voluntary prayer to our schools.". . . He intended to provide children the opportunity of sharing in their spiritual heritage of Alabama and of this country. . . . [Therefore, the statute is] invalid because the sole purpose . . . was an effort on the part of the state of Alabama to encourage a religious activity. . . . [It] is a law respecting the establishment of religion within the meaning of the First Amendment.[56]

"SECULARISM NEVER SLEEPS"?

The ongoing debate over prayer in the public schools has divided the country into two opposing camps. This statement, issued in 1994 by Don Feder of the Christian Coalition, a conservative religious lobbying group, clearly expresses the frustration and outrage of those who feel that school prayer and other classroom religious activities have been unfairly and unwisely suppressed in the long wake of *Engel v. Vitale* and should be reinstated for the good of the country.

> The classroom is a major arena in the ongoing clash of values. Secularists have made it so. Since 1962, when the Supreme Court declared [in *Engel v. Vitale*] the Supreme Being *persona non grata* [unwelcome] in the school house, we've seen an escalating attack on all forms of religion in public life. The Court has been relentless, prohibiting prayer, Bible-reading, a moment of silence, and even the posting of the Ten Commandments on a school bulletin board. . . . The Judiciary is ably assisted by battalions of bureaucrats, educrats, and self-appointed guardians of the wall of separation [between church and state]. In Jackson, Mississippi, a principal was fired (later reinstated) for allowing students to read a prayer over the intercom. In Missouri, a student got detention for praying over his lunch. . . . A second-grader in upstate New York was told the storybook she brought to share with her class was "inappropriate" because it contained the dreaded G-word [God]. . . . When it comes to ferreting out religious expression, secularism never sleeps. . . . As traditional values, which once were the core of public education, have been driven from their fortified positions, secular dogmas have occupied those battlements.

Many of those who were critical of the Court's *Wallace v. Jaffree* ruling accused the federal government of continuing an erosion of the religious rights of Americans, an erosion that had begun with the 1962 *Engel* ruling. They expressed strong agreement with Chief Justice Warren Burger, who dissented in the *Jaffree* case. "It makes no sense," Burger declared,

> to say that Alabama has "endorsed prayer" by merely enacting a new statute "to specify expressly that voluntary prayer is one of the authorized activities during a moment of silence" [as stated in the Alabama law]. . . . To suggest that a moment of silence statute that includes the word "prayer" unconstitutionally endorses religion, while one that simply provides for a moment of silence does not, manifests not neutrality but hostility toward religion. . . . The notion that the Alabama statute is a step toward creating an established church borders on, if it does not trespass into, the ridiculous. The statute does not remotely threaten religious liberty. . . . It accommodates the purely private, voluntary religious choices of the individual pupils who wish to pray while at the same time creating a time for non-religious reflection for those who do not choose to pray.[57]

Prayer Is Banned from Graduation Ceremonies

The limits of school prayer were tested and clarified once again by the Supreme Court in the 1992 *Lee v. Weisman* case. The Court's majority opinion itself summed up the background facts:

> The city of Providence, Rhode Island, had a policy permitting its public high school and middle school principals to invite members of the clergy to offer invocation and benediction prayers as part of the school's formal graduation ceremonies. Pursuant to this policy, the principal of the middle school invited a rabbi to offer such prayers. The principal . . . advised the rabbi that the invocation and benediction should be nonsectarian [not derived from or aimed at any single religious sect].[58]

Senator Jesse Helms of North Carolina (right) was one of many lawmakers who tried to legalize school prayer.

A Providence resident, Daniel Weisman, took issue with the benediction, saying that his daughter, Deborah, a graduating student, was being forced to listen to a prayer she did not endorse. He filed suit, attempting to prohibit the recital of prayers at all public-school graduation and promotional activities. Relying heavily on the reasoning of the 1962 *Engel* ruling, the High Court favored Weisman's position in a five to four vote, saying, "It is not enough that the government restrain [school authorities] from compelling [students to take part in] religious practices. It must not engage in them either."[59] Using similar reasoning, in the 1996 *Nartowicz v. Clayton* case, the Court ruled that devotionals at school assemblies and school-sponsored events are similarly unconstitutional.

Lawmakers Attempt to Legalize School Prayer

During the 1980s and 1990s, court cases were not the only attempts to challenge or clarify the Supreme Court's rulings. Lawmakers and politicians also kept the issue of school prayer alive. Long after Congressman Frank Becker's proposed constitutional amendment failed to pass in the mid-1960s, other legislators, usually backed by conservative religious groups, mounted attempts to pass similar amendments. In 1982, for instance, at the suggestion of President Ronald Reagan, some U.S. senators held a hearing on the matter; but for various reasons, this initiative went no further. The following year Republican senators Jesse Helms (North Carolina) and Strom Thurmond (South Carolina) reintroduced the amendment; but in 1984 the Senate voted it down.

Another tactic some members of Congress tried was to tie the hands of the Supreme Court by passing legislation using the same words and phrases that would appear in a constitutional amendment. If the bill passed, these pro-prayer phrases would become law, and unless someone challenged the law, the Supreme Court would have no opportunity to intervene. In 1979, for example, Senator Helms introduced legislation in which he referred specifically to the *Engel* case. The bill read, in part,

> Nothing in this Constitution shall be construed to prohibit individual or group prayer in public schools or other public institutions. No person shall be required by the United States or by any state to participate in prayer. Neither the United States nor any state shall compose the words of any prayer to be said in public schools.[60]

Helms stated in the Senate, "Until the right of voluntary prayer is restored, we will continue to have officially sanctioned discrimination against collective worship."[61] He claimed that he was promoting tolerance and fairness and that he hoped it would ultimately be the voters, and not the Supreme Court, who would decide the school prayer issue. Although his bill passed in the Senate, it failed in the House, and the legislation fizzled.

Another tactic, which aimed to limit the Supreme Court's power and clarify which religious activities on school campuses would be acceptable, was the passage of the Equal Access Act in 1984. The act declared that noncurriculum-related student groups could meet on secondary school campuses during noninstructional times and that schools could not deny equal access to or discriminate against students who wished to conduct a meeting. Discrimination on the basis of religious, political, philosophical, or other content of the speech employed by these student groups would violate the Equal Access Act. Therefore, any students wishing to engage in prayer during these informal, noninstructional meetings held outside of the classroom could do so.

The law was worded carefully to avoid the issues addressed by judges in the *Engel, Schempp, Weisman*, and other similar cases in hopes of ensuring that the courts could not invalidate it based on these past cases. For instance, the law stipulates that the student meetings must be completely voluntary and student-run. In no way can they be directed or run by nonschool persons. Also, the school was forbidden to influence the content of prayers or the activities of religious clubs meeting on campus, to require anyone to participate, or financially to sponsor any such club, apart from providing the meeting space.

The Battle Lines Are Still Drawn

Despite the passage of the Equal Access Act, many Americans continued to accuse the federal government, and the Supreme Court

---

As long as student prayer groups are voluntary and student-run and schools allow equal access, it is legal for students to pray on school grounds.

A HIGH-SCHOOL GRADUATION TURNS SOUR

Numerous controversies of one sort or another over school prayer occur each year, but most never make it to local courts, much less to the Supreme Court. This is one recent example, reported by the Associated Press on May 28, 1999.

No one was supposed to pray at Northern High School's graduation [in Silver Springs, Maryland]. Student Nick Becker, the ACLU, and the state attorney general's office had persuaded Calvert County officials to observe 30 seconds of silence instead. . . . During the period of silence in the May 26 [1999] ceremony, a man began reciting the Lord's Prayer aloud. Virtually the entire 4,000-member audience joined in. Becker left, then tried to return, but was stopped by Maryland state police. . . . "I told the cop I'm getting my diploma," Becker told the *Washington Post*. . . . "He said 'you're not going back in.' He walked me over to the car, put me in the front of the patrol car, and said he was going to give me a citation for failing to obey a lawful order.". . . Becker objected [to the prayer], saying that prayer doesn't belong in a public [school] ceremony. The ACLU of Maryland and the attorney general's office told Calvert officials that prayer at graduation violates the constitutional separation of church and state. . . . ACLU spokeswoman Suzanne Smith said detaining Becker was tantamount to arresting him. "The real loser here is the Constitution and the right of people to express dissent," she said.

in particular, of harboring animosity toward religion and religious expression. Hoping to quell such criticisms and promote an atmosphere of tolerance on both sides of the issue, in 1995 President Bill Clinton drafted a memorandum and sent it to both the U.S. attorney general and the secretary of education. The memorandum read, in part,

Nothing in the First Amendment converts our public schools into religion-free zones, or requires all religious expression to be left behind at the schoolhouse door. While the government may not use schools to coerce the consciences of our students or to convey official endorsement of religion, the government's schools also may not discriminate against private religious expression during the day. . . . The First Amendment permits and protects a greater degree of religious expression in public schools than many Americans may now understand.[62]

One result of Clinton's memorandum was a set of guidelines published in April 1995 by a coalition of religious and civil liberties organizations in a pamphlet titled "Religion in the Public Schools:

President Bill Clinton attempted to promote tolerance by drafting a memorandum which addressed both sides of the school prayer issue.

A Joint Statement of Current Law." Cited was the fact that students have the right to engage in individual or group prayer and religious discussion during the day. For example, they may say grace before meals, pray before tests, and read their Bibles and other religious books. Moreover, though local authorities possess substantial discretion to impose rules of order, they may not discriminate against religious activity or speech.

Clearly, the school policies and students' rights mentioned in these guidelines were very general. Like the court cases that preceded them, they did not deal with every possible situation in which prayer might arise on public-school grounds. This was illustrated dramatically in the June 2000 Supreme Court decision in *Santa Fe Independent School District v. Jane Doe*, a case involving school prayer in Galveston, Texas. For quite some time, the Santa Fe School District in that city had allowed student-initiated and student-led prayers to be broadcast over school public-address systems prior to football games. The mothers of two local students (who were not named in the court papers), one Catholic, the other

---

Santa Fe High School's practice of broadcasting student-led prayer over the public-address system was challenged in court.

Mormon, filed suit, and the Supreme Court eventually voted six to three in their favor. Justice John P. Stevens delivered the majority opinion, which read, in part,

> We recognize the important role that public worship plays in many communities, as well as the sincere desire to include public prayer as a part of various occasions so as to mark those occasions' significance. But such religious activities in public schools, as elsewhere, must comport with the First Amendment. . . . Even if we regard every high school student's decision to attend a home football game as purely voluntary, we are nevertheless persuaded that the delivery of a pre-game prayer has the improper effect of coercing those present to participate in an act of religious worship.[63]

This case shows that, nearly forty years after the Supreme Court made its famous ruling in the *Engel v. Vitale* case, school prayer remains a relevant, controversial, and potentially divisive issue. The battle lines are still drawn between those who want to see prayer remain a private act barred from public schools and those who desire that prayer be reinstated in public schools. And it is still far from clear which side will ultimately win.

Notes

Introduction: Banning School Prayer Raises Larger Issues

1. Quoted in John H. Laubach, *School Prayers: Congress, the Courts, and the Public*. Washington, DC: Public Affairs, 1969, pp. 1–2.
2. Sam Duker, *The Public Schools and Religion: The Legal Context*. New York: Harper and Row, 1966, pp. 14–15.

Chapter 1: The Establishment of Religious Practices in American Schools

3. Quoted in Duker, *The Public Schools and Religion*, p. 159.
4. Quoted in Diane Ravitch, ed., *The American Reader: Words That Moved a Nation*. New York: HarperCollins, 1990, p. 24.
5. *Zorach v. Clauson*, 343 U.S. 306, 313.
6. Quoted in David Barton, *Original Intent: The Courts, the Constitution, and Religion*. Aledo, TX: Wallbuilder, 1997, p. 56.
7. Quoted in Barton, *Original Intent*, p. 56.
8. Quoted in Barton, *Original Intent*, pp. 57–58.

Chapter 2: The New York Courts Consider a Protest Against School Prayer

9. Quoted in Laubach, *School Prayers*, p. 40.
10. Quoted in Duker, *The Public Schools and Religion*, p. 150.
11. Quoted in Duker, *The Public Schools and Religion*, p. 151.
12. Quoted in Duker, *The Public Schools and Religion*, p. 151.
13. Quoted in Duker, *The Public Schools and Religion*, pp. 152–53.
14. Quoted in Duker, *The Public Schools and Religion*, p. 154.
15. Quoted in Duker, *The Public Schools and Religion*, pp. 157–58.

Chapter 3: The Supreme Court Hears the Case

16. Oral Arguments for *Engel v. Vitale*, Supreme Court, April 3, 1962. Real Audio. http://oyez.nwu.edu/cases/cases.cgi?command=show&case_id=111.
17. Oral Arguments for *Engel v. Vitale*.
18. Oral Arguments for *Engel v. Vitale*.
19. Oral Arguments for *Engel v. Vitale*.

20. Oral Arguments for *Engel v. Vitale.*
21. Oral Arguments for *Engel v. Vitale.*
22. Oral Arguments for *Engel v. Vitale.*
23. Oral Arguments for *Engel v. Vitale.*
24. Oral Arguments for *Engel v. Vitale.*
25. Oral Arguments for *Engel v. Vitale.*
26. Oral Arguments for *Engel v. Vitale.*
27. Oral Arguments for *Engel v. Vitale.*
28. Oral Arguments for *Engel v. Vitale.*
29. Oral Arguments for *Engel v. Vitale.*
30. Oral Arguments for *Engel v. Vitale.*

Chapter 4: The High Court Decides in Favor of the Petitioners

31. Hugo Black, majority opinion in *Engel v. Vitale*, 370 U.S. 421 (1962).
32. Black, majority opinion.
33. Black, majority opinion.
34. Quoted in Black, majority opinion.
35. Black, majority opinion.
36. Black, majority opinion.
37. William O. Douglas, concurring opinion in *Engel v. Vitale*, 370 U.S. 421 (1962).
38. Douglas, concurring opinion.
39. Douglas, concurring opinion.
40. Douglas, concurring opinion.
41. Potter Stewart, dissenting opinion in *Engel v. Vitale*, 370 U.S. 421 (1962).
42. Stewart, dissenting opinion.
43. Stewart, dissenting opinion.
44. Stewart, dissenting opinion.
45. Black, majority opinion.

Chapter 5: The Court's Decision Stirs Up Controversy

46. Quoted in *Time*, "The Supreme Court to Stand as a Guarantee," July 6, 1962, p. 8.
47. Quoted in *Christian Science Monitor*, "Prayer Ruling Debated," June 26, 1962, p. 4.

48. Quoted in Laubach, *School Prayers*, p. 63.
49. Quoted in Alexander Burnham, "Edict Is Called a Setback by Christian Clerics," *New York Times*, June 26, 1962, p. 17.
50. Quoted in Fred Hechinger, "Many States Use Prayer in School," *New York Times*, June 26, 1962, p. 17.
51. Quoted in *New York Times*, "Regent's Prayer in Public Schools Is Outlawed by Supreme Court," June 26, 1962, p. A1+.
52. Quoted in *New York Times*, "Regent's Prayer in Public Schools Is Outlawed by Supreme Court," p. A1+.
53. Quoted in Burnham, "Edict Is Called a Setback by Christian Clerics," p. 1.
54. Quoted in Laubach, *School Prayers*, p. 47.
55. Quoted in Laubach, *School Prayers*, p. 45.

Chapter 6: The War over Prayer in the Schools Continues

56. Quoted in Barton, *Original Intent*, p. 176.
57. Quoted in Barton, *Original Intent*, pp. 178–79.
58. Antonin Scalia, dissenting opinion in *Lee v. Weisman*, 120 L. Ed. 2nd 467, 529 (1992).
59. Harry Blackmun, concurring opinion in *Lee v. Weisman*, 120 L. Ed. 2nd 467, 529 (1992).
60. Quoted in *Senate Record*, 98th Cong., 2nd sess., March 20, 1984.
61. Quoted in *Senate Record*.
62. Quoted in *New York Times*, "Text of President Clinton's Memorandum on Religion in the Schools," July 13, 1995.
63. Quoted in *New York Times*, June 19, 2000.

For Further Reading

Isaac Asimov, *The Birth of the United States, 1763–1816*. Boston: Houghton Mifflin, 1974. One of the most popular writers of the twentieth century here delivers a highly informative survey of the main events and characters of the early decades of the United States, touching on the First Amendment and freedom of religion.

Carol Haas, *"Engel v. Vitale": Separation of Church and State*. Hillside, NJ: Enslow, 1994. A general synopsis of the case and the larger issue of separation of church and state surrounding it.

Debbie Levy, *Civil Liberties*. San Diego: Lucent Books, 2000. This concise overview of American freedoms contains a useful chapter on religion and school prayer.

Don Nardo, *The Bill of Rights*. San Diego: Greenhaven, 1998. Examines the Bill of Rights, including the First Amendment, in an opposing-viewpoints format and a clear, easy-to-read style.

———, *The Declaration of Independence: A Model for Individual Rights*. San Diego: Lucent Books, 1999. Describes the atmosphere surrounding the founding fathers during the crucial formative years of the United States, including Jefferson's ideas about freedom and government.

Works Consulted

Books

Robert S. Alley, ed., *The Supreme Court on Church and State*. New York: Oxford University Press, 1988. An effective summary of the High Court's decisions relating to the church-and-state issue up to that time.

David Barton, *America's Godly Heritage*. Aledo, TX: Wallbuilder, 1990. Barton summarizes the many religious traditions and institutions of the United States, among them school prayer and Bible readings.

———, *Original Intent: The Courts, the Constitution, and Religion*. Aledo, TX: Wallbuilder, 1997. In this extremely well-researched book, Barton makes the case that the Supreme Court has erred in many of its rulings that have restricted prayer and other religious practices in the schools.

Archibald Cox, *The Court and the Constitution*. Boston: Houghton Mifflin, 1987. Cox, a noted legal scholar, explores how constitutional matters have fared in the courts over the years.

Kenneth M. Dolbeare and Phillip E. Hammond, *The School Prayer Decisions: From Court Policy to Local Practice*. Chicago: University of Chicago Press, 1971. The authors offer a summary of the major school prayer court cases up to 1970 as well as data about compliance by school systems.

William O. Douglas, *The Court Years, 1939–1975*. New York: Random House, 1980. The man who wrote the concurring opinion in the *Engel v. Vitale* case in 1962 recalls his experiences in First Amendment–related and other cases that came before him on the High Court.

Sam Duker, *The Public Schools and Religion: The Legal Context*. New York: Harper and Row, 1966. This summary of important cases involving religious practices in schools is valuable because it provides full or fulsome quotes from the Supreme Court opinions on many of these cases.

John H. Laubach, *School Prayers: Congress, the Courts, and the Public*. Washington, DC: Public Affairs, 1969. A very detailed and useful summary and analysis of the *Engel, Schempp*, and other related cases of the 1960s as well as Congressman Becker's ill-fated attempt to create a school-prayer amendment to the Constitution.

James E. Leahy, *The First Amendment, 1791–1991*. Jefferson, NC: McFarland, 1991. An excellent synopsis of the historical issues surrounding the First Amendment and the issues of freedom of speech, press, and religion.

Richard E. Morgan, *The Supreme Court and Religion*. New York: Free, 1972. This well-written volume discusses cases involving religion during the nineteenth century and the free exercise and establishment clauses in the twentieth century.

Diane Ravitch, ed., *The American Reader: Words That Moved a Nation*. New York: HarperCollins, 1990. An excellent collection of important documents from American history.

William Rehnquist, *The Supreme Court: How It Was, How It Is*. New York: Morrow, 1997. An excellent insight into the workings of the Supreme Court.

Tamara L. Roleff, ed., *Civil Liberties: Opposing Viewpoints*. San Diego: Greenhaven, 1999. Offers current commentary reflecting both sides of the issue of separation of church and state.

Frank Sorauf, *The Wall of Separation*. Princeton, NJ: Princeton University Press, 1976. Examines the issues and outcomes in over sixty American court cases relating to the subject of separation of church and state.

John W. Whitehead, *The Rights of Religious Persons in Public Education*. Wheaton, IL: Crossway Books, 1991. This book comes out in favor of expanded religious rights for teachers and students in public schools and is somewhat critical of Supreme Court rulings that it sees as having curtailed these rights, including *Engel v. Vitale*.

Elder Witt, *The Supreme Court and Individual Rights*. Washington, DC: Congressional Quarterly, 1988. A spirited discussion of the High Court's decisions relating to basic American freedoms.

Periodicals

Alexander Burnham, "Edict Is Called a Setback by Christian Clerics," *New York Times*, June 26, 1962.

Christian Science Monitor, "Prayer Ruling Debated,"June 26, 1962.

Fred Hechinger, "Many States Use Prayer in School," *New York Times,* June 26, 1962.

New York Times, "Prayer Is Personal," June 27, 1962.

————, "Regents Prayer in Public Schools Is Outlawed by Supreme Court," June 26, 1962.

————, "Text of President Clinton's Memorandum on Religion in the Schools," July 13, 1995.

Time, "The Supreme Court to Stand as a Guarantee," July 6, 1962.

Wall Street Journal, "In the Name of Freedom," June 27, 1962.

H. Frank Way, "Survey Research on Judicial Decisions: The Prayer and Bible Reading Cases," *Western Political Quarterly,* June 1968.

Internet Source

Oral Arguments for *Engel v. Vitale,* Supreme Court, April 3, 1962. Real Audio. http://oyez.nwu.edu/cases/cases.cgi?command= show&case_id=111.

Index

91

Picture Credits

Cover photo: © Bettmann/Corbis
© James L. Amos/Corbis, 69
AP Photo/Benoit, 26
AP Photo/Michael Stravato, 82
Archive Photos, 52
© Bettmann/Corbis, 8, 16, 17, 23, 31, 58, 65, 70, 71, 74, 77, 79
Brown Brothers, 21, 48, 61
© FPG International, 44, 66
Lambert/Archive Photos, 35
Library of Congress, 14, 45, 53, 64
© Jonathan Meyers/FPG International, 81
Prints Old and Rare, 41
© John A. Rizzo/PhotoDisc, 30
© Lee Snider/Corbis, 19
© Mike Valeri/FPG International, 11
© Oscar White/Corbis, 51, 56
© Adam Woolfitt/Corbis, 39
© Jack Zehrt/FPG International, 55

About the Author

Julia C. Loren is a native of California. After a sojourn in Seattle, Washington, where she obtained a degree in Editorial Journalism from the University of Washington, she worked as a newspaper reporter and editor for several years. She also has a Master's degree in Community Counseling and Family Therapy from Seattle Pacific University.

She is the author of a book for teenagers called *The Note on the Mirror–Pregnant Teens Tell Their Stories* (Zondervan, 1990). She also authored a series of books on adoption for counseling professionals and women's self-help (Adoption Counsel Press, 1999–2000). At present, Julia lives in San Diego, California, where she works as a freelance writer and new media marketing consultant.